# ISAIAH'S STORY

JENNIFER ROSS

# ISAIAH'S STORY

JENNIFER ROSS

AMBASSADOR INTERNATIONAL
GREENVILLE, SOUTH CAROLINA & BELFAST, NORTHERN IRELAND

www.ambassador-international.com

# ISAIAH'S STORY

© 2014 by Jennifer Ross
All rights reserved

Printed in the United States of America

ISBN: 978-1-62020-251-7
eISBN: 978-1-62020-351-4

Cover design and typesetting: David Siglin
E-book conversion: Anna Riebe

Unless otherwise noted, all Scripture is from the King James Version. Public Domain.

AMBASSADOR INTERNATIONAL
Emerald House
427 Wade Hampton Blvd.
Greenville, SC 29609, USA
www.ambassador-international.com

AMBASSADOR BOOKS
The Mount
2 Woodstock Link
Belfast, BT6 8DD, Northern Ireland, UK
www.ambassador-international.com

*The colophon is a trademark of Ambassador*

# DEDICATION

In loving memory of my son

Isaiah Christopher Ross

This book was written to give life to the life that you didn't get to live.

# Foreword

*by Andrea Rodgers, writer and mother*

I first became aware of Isaiah's story in March 2009. I was a stay-at-home mom of a son who was not quite one year old at the time. As I visited various blogs one afternoon, I came across a prayer request for Jennifer Ross, a mother of three boys at home, one in heaven, and one in her womb. Jennifer was at risk of losing her new baby for the same reason that she'd lost Isaiah seven months before. I couldn't imagine losing one child, let alone two—and in one year!

Immediately, I began praying.

I saw that Jennifer had a blog, so I added it to my bookmarks to visit each day and let her know that she was on my mind. Week after week, I thought about this amazing woman during my mornings, afternoons, and nights. Her faith in God was so inspiring. She didn't waver with her trust and praise in the Lord. She did not let her experiences make her bitter. She was a great Christian example. It was a miracle when her doctor declared her pregnancy was healthy and that her fifth son would be okay!

As I began to learn more about Isaiah, the little boy who'd gone to heaven too soon, my heart broke for Jennifer's loss. It would have been easier and less painful for me to stop reading. Most of her blog visitors were other mothers who had gone through the same thing. What did I have to offer? I could not identify—it was a world that I, honestly, wanted to pretend didn't exist. I'd had one pregnancy at the time—and he was my world. I couldn't imagine anything worse than to watch my child pass away. And yet, I felt God push me to keep reading. I had plenty I could learn from Jennifer.

I'd always felt a special connection to those who dealt with miscarriages and prematurity. My mom had suffered four miscarriages, and I was born at thirty weeks gestation. To me, a baby was just as sacred in the womb at nine weeks or nine months.

At the same time, I never thought about the long-term grief process. For centuries (because it was so common to lose a baby), there was a mentality that the loss, especially preterm, was better left not talked about. It was a private pain—and something that time and other children would heal.

I now know this couldn't be farther from the truth. Due to Jennifer opening herself up to share her grief in the years that followed the death of Isaiah, I understand that it's just as important to acknowledge and celebrate the lives of infants who have passed, as if they had been with us for many years.

When I was twelve, I knew a woman who experienced this devastation a month before her due date because the umbilical cord had wrapped around her daughter's neck. Every year on their Christmas cards, they acknowledge their angel. That baby will always be a part of their family. They went on to raise four children, but they think of their missing daughter every day and do not hide from it. Her death is not shameful, nor should anyone else forget that she was a perfectly formed, healthy little girl.

Since then, I have crossed paths with other families who have lost premature babies—including in my own extended family. Knowing Isaiah's story has helped me to be able to be there for others, as infant loss is never going to go away. Even with our wonderful advancements in the medical field, there are situations that cannot be avoided—such as in Jennifer's case.

We are not meant to stick together with only those who know the same heartaches as we do. At the same time, families who have experienced a similar situation will find wonderful comfort and inspiration through Jennifer's beautiful and talented writing of Isaiah's story.

I have been in awe of her selflessness, her strength, and her determination not to let the darkness take over, but rather to honor her son. Isaiah may have only breathed for a short time, but he has a purpose in this world. He has touched many lives in different ways.

It was a dreary, rainy evening when I sat down on my couch with my laptop to read this book. As I read about the rainbow being Jennifer's symbol for Isaiah, I noticed a burst of sunlight through my window. It was so sudden and strong that I glanced up to see where it had come from. When I looked back down at my computer, I gasped. A rainbow was across my screen.

I had to set my laptop aside to cry for a moment. *Isaiah! You know I'm reading your story! Thank you for introducing yourself to me!*

I felt so blessed to have connected with him. It was an incredible moment that I will never forget for the rest of my life. A reminder to me that we are not far from our loved ones on the other side. Life doesn't make sense—especially when it comes to the death of a child. But, faith is believing that someday we will understand. Someday we will have the answers. Until then, we are given signs to keep holding on . . . it's simply a matter of whether we take notice. I noticed, Isaiah. Thank you.

# Doctor's Note

*by Eve Rider, D.O.*

We knew this pregnancy was at risk for the last two months. Suddenly, not only was the pregnancy at risk, but so was the mother.

The condition started as a retro placental hematoma, or a blood clot between the placenta and its attachment to the vital blood vessels of the uterus. It had suddenly enlarged to twice the size and encompassed over half of the placental surface. Jennifer had presented to the hospital with a large amount of bleeding this time. Her labs showed she was in DIC. A medical condition where the body's own cells are using up its own blood clotting system, so the body will bleed to death internally. This carries a greater than 50% chance of death.

If Jennifer didn't continue to progress in labor rapidly, she would die. And the delivery itself posed a risk of blood loss that we couldn't control.

The chance of this child surviving to where he could live outside his mother's womb was minimal; that was another six weeks away. Jennifer's body didn't have another day if we didn't get the placenta out. It was the root of the DIC. She had to deliver this pregnancy, or she and her baby would die. Even with the blood products we were giving her, she could still die.

Hoping for alternatives, but knowing there were none, I called my perinatal colleagues. They confirmed that there were no other alternatives if we wanted to save this mother's life.

We had to deliver this boy from his mother . . .

# Chapter 1

As I recline in my bed, I look down at the movement of my violet maternity top. To view the movement clearly, I lift the bottom of my shirt up and over the bump that safely nestles my baby. A smile washes over my tired face as I place my hand upon that little boy dancing in my womb. I can feel the happiness and joy that fills his spirit.

This is my fourth time experiencing the beauty of pregnancy, and with each pregnancy, I am continually amazed at the miraculous work of our Lord's hands. I enjoy every flip, kick, and hiccup. Truly cherish every minute while my baby shows off for me, his proud mommy.

Yet within minutes, with my back propped against a pile of soft pillows, fear takes hold of the smile that had covered my face. I place my hands on my mattress, lifting myself into a sitting position. My ears start to ring, and my sight starts to blur. With my heart racing, I begin to fear the worst. An early arrival for my unborn baby.

Panic overtakes me as I stand to my feet. Pressure consumes my abdomen. I begin to feel the pain that occurs right before the body prepares for birth, a pain I've felt prior to three other births. A phone has become first priority.

As I make my way out of the bedroom, holding myself up with the dresser and trailing along the wall of the hallway, I keep repeating the words, "Oh God, please help me, please."

I get to a phone and dial my husband's cell number. He's out picking up some items at the local grocer. I frantically tell him that something is wrong and that I need help right now! I'm too frightened to wait for him to arrive home in time to get me to the hospital. Knowing that he is on his way home, I hang up and immediately dial 9-1-1.

With the operator on the phone, I try to get the words out as quickly as possible. I give my name and address before giving the reason for the emergency. I beg for someone to get to my house as soon as possible. The operator stays on the line as I grab my cell phone off the kitchen counter and call my mother. At this point, my speech becomes a whispering shriek. "Something is wrong with me, Mom! Go to the hospital!" I stand in my living room, holding the arm of my couch, not able to fully stand or sit down.

In a far off distance, I can hear the siren blaring down the driveway. As the sound gets closer, I can visualize the red flashing lights ricocheting off the siding as neighbors curiously peep out their windows.

Standing in the living room with shadows of darkness all around me, the fear of death fills my every thought. How could this be happening?

The sound of hard-soled boots echoes through the corridor as the paramedic crew rushes up the staircase to my front door. Finally, my help has arrived.

I am placed on the end of the couch, right where I had clung to the arm minutes earlier. My entire body begins to shake. I cannot move voluntarily.

The legs of the stretcher are dropped and the wheels locked into place. With a paramedic to my right and left, my arms are embraced with their strength. Almost effortlessly, they place me onto the cold hard gurney.

My body feels as if it has gone into some sort of frozen state. I cannot lay my legs straight or my back down, and yet all that occupies my mind is that little boy joyfully dancing around inside of me. Had my adrenaline traveled through his blood? Could he feel my fear?

The crew of medics makes sure that I am safely secured, and they carry me slowly down a flight of stairs and out into the frigid air. My husband has arrived to stay with the boys until my stepdad, Keith, can take his place. The boys never wake up from all of the noise going on in the living room. As soon as Keith arrives, my husband takes off to be with me at the hospital.

Inside the ambulance, the stretcher is locked into place, and the heavy ambulance doors are shut with force. Above the sound of the blaring siren, I can hear the driver communicating with the hospital over the radio, letting the nurses and doctors know that I will be arriving shortly.

On the way to the hospital, my vital signs are checked repeatedly. With my jaw shaking and teeth chattering, I ask the woman in the back of the ambulance if I can hold her hand. Subconsciously, I hope that by holding her hand, my body's shaking will come to a halt. The attempt fails.

Through the darkness of night, rounding the street corners and speeding over bumps down the highway, we not only begin our journey to the hospital, but a new journey is about to begin in my life.

Little did I know then that my dreams for a complete family, healthy and whole, would be thrown into the air like the gravel that flew out from underneath the back wheels of the ambulance. It was a trip I never prepared for. One I never wanted to take.

Thus, my journey begins . . .

# CHAPTER 2

I can remember a fun activity I enjoyed every year in elementary school. One year in particular, I can still visualize the word *Mom* scribbled on dotted paper.

It was my first grade year. I can still smell that brand new box of shiny crayons. I remember carefully tipping the box over and lining each crayon up with the untouched tips of color all facing the same direction. With the art skills of a first grader, I began to draw a tall, lanky stick figure. That was the picture that I proudly drew above that one simple word, *Mom*. That image is permanently etched in my mind as if it were yesterday.

The goal behind this activity was to share what career we wanted to pursue as an adult. That was easy for me. A mother. That is all I have ever wanted to be in life. Not a doctor, lawyer, or astronaut. I just wanted to stay home and be with my children. That is what my mother chose to do, and I was going to do the same. I wanted to have a large family with lots of children. As it turns out, that is exactly what I did.

My husband, Chris, and I had each experienced a failed marriage prior to meeting and eventually sharing vows with one another on June 7, 2002. We also became stepparents that day—I to Nicholas, and Chris to Caleb.

When it came to family planning, Chris and I put our trust in the Lord. We knew and believed that the Lord would provide for our every need. We have always lived from paycheck to paycheck. However, I can say without hesitation that we have had every necessity met. We have never gone without food, clothes, or all that is required for a healthy living environment.

In Genesis, the first book of the Bible, you'll find the words "Be fruitful, and multiply" written in chapter one. I have heard those words preached over and over again. I believe that every word written in the Bible is holy and complete truth. My husband and I obeyed God and happily began adding precious children to our family.

By the age of twenty-three, I had carried and given birth to three healthy, beautiful boys. Caleb William, Devon Garrett, and Parker John. My body took a much-needed break from pregnancy for a few years. Then in January 2008, I discovered through a store-bought pregnancy test that we were expecting again. I was thrilled! Sadly, after a couple of weeks, my body miscarried that sweet baby. I was deeply saddened. I had never experienced a miscarriage, and quite honestly, I never thought that it would happen to me. I allowed my body to heal for one month before my husband and I began to try for another baby. Not a replacement for the child lost. We were simply bound and determined to continue adding to our growing family.

In March 2008, I took a pregnancy test before I was due for my menstrual cycle. I just knew that deep within my womb, without our knowledge, we had a new family member on the way. I remember being filled with excitement as I watched that light pink line form through the result window on the pregnancy test. Once again, I felt extremely blessed and was so very thankful to be entrusted with this child formed by our God's hands. Joy filled my heart.

I called and made the appointment to see my doctor for my eight-week check-up. That call was followed by endless calls to my family and friends. I shared the due date, December 25, 2008, and our excitement for this child. They embraced our news with best wishes for our family.

After a short time, I became very nervous about this pregnancy because of the miscarriage I had experienced in January. Five weeks into my pregnancy, I called and requested to see the doctor sooner. They understood my concern and had me see the doctor that same morning. I could not wait to see that growing baby on the black and white ultrasound screen, and of course I wanted to make sure that the sac that held the baby had implanted properly into the wall of my uterus.

When I arrived at the doctor's office, a nurse took me to the back, made sure that I was comfortable, and began to prepare me for my ultrasound. A few minutes later, the doctor greeted me with a cheerful hello. He wasn't my usual doctor but was willing to see me because my doctor was not available to see me that morning. He applied some gel to my belly and began to perform the ultrasound.

Without blinking, I watched that little square screen for that very first glimpse of my precious child. It only took seconds, and then this tiny body appeared.

I was so wrapped up in watching the constant movement of the baby's body and strong healthy heart beat that it took me a minute to realize that the doctor was not speaking. I turned toward the doctor, assuming that his body language would help me identify the reason behind his silence.

He was closely examining my uterus on the ultrasound. His finger moved up to the screen to point out some concerning findings. He ran his hand over a black area above the sac. It was fresh blood. The bleed was directly over the placenta. The doctor began to explain the imposing danger that this was going to cause my baby. He stated that a little spot of blood could be normal after implantation, but not the amount that he was seeing around my baby. The appointment ended with the doctor explaining that the large amount of blood taking over the placenta would eventually cause the baby to be malnourished, causing the baby to be miscarried soon after. He printed me off some pictures of my ultrasound and told me to call with any questions or problems. He walked out of the room to continue on with his list of patients, and I quietly removed my gown and put my clothes back on.

I remember walking out of that room and down the short hallway to the waiting room. Around the room sat pregnant women holding their growing bellies. I too sat there three times over, holding and rubbing my growing baby belly. I was in total disbelief of this unsettling news. I had my mind set that I was to have the next miracle baby in my hometown. I walked out of that hospital, filling myself with my own strength, not realizing that soon I would be clinging to the Lord's strength.

# CHAPTER 3

In the following weeks of my pregnancy, I had ultrasound upon ultrasound done. Each week brought an increased amount of new blood that was forming and embedding in the placenta. As the pooling of blood around the amniotic sac increased, so did my worry for my unborn child.

My doctor, Eve Rider, had been absolutely wonderful as I visited often for check-ups in her office. She did not feel the need to have me on bed rest. She said that the bleeding taking place inside my uterus would continue no matter what activity I chose to do, whether it be housework, grocery shopping, or playing with my children outside. She felt it best that I keep up with daily activities so that my body would stay strong.

I never took it upon myself to order my own bed rest. To this day, I struggle with wishing that I had. I look at many options that I could have tried, but I did not do anything. I chose to trust wholly in the Lord's will and prayed daily that my body would fend for this child until the weeks of viability arrived. I was so close to twenty-four weeks gestation. I knew that is where I needed to be in my pregnancy before this baby would have a sliver of a chance to survive.

I did a lot of research on the Internet regarding premature birth. The March of Dimes had a lot of good information available. I was able to learn about the difficulties that occur during the weeks of an early birth, leading up to a full-term baby. After studying this website, I understood the conditions and hazards that my child faced. It was too much for my heart to carry, so I quickly put those statistics to the back of my mind.

I continued to take care of my health the best I knew how. I ate healthy foods, stayed active, and took time to rest when needed. My hope began to grow around week twelve. An ultrasound showed that the old blood was forming into clotted tissue as the blood began to age. The doctor had a positive, upbeat reaction to this news. She rolled her chair closer to mine and pointed out the location of the blood clot. With her pencil in hand, she marked out a route in which the clot might travel and safely exit through the cervix as the baby grew within my uterus.

My favorite part of that appointment was when I talked the ultrasound technician into guessing the baby's gender. I knew that the prediction would not carry a 100% guarantee that early in the pregnancy, but I was happily willing to trust a guess at a 90% guarantee! I can still see that woman's porcelain smile, eclipsed through the rays of light that omitted off the screen, as she searched for my answer. While looking, she asked the gender of my other children. "All boys," I answered with a playful laugh. She laughed along with me and replied, "It looks like you are having another little boy!" We both giggled together like a couple of schoolgirls. Pure joy echoed throughout that little room as we shared in my special moment.

I smile proudly as I think back on the doctor saying in an amazed tone, "How perfect this babe looks!" Yes, I was the proud mom indeed. It reminds me of those moments when you have this overwhelming sense of love for your child. For me, it was such a beautiful moment, filled with much-needed hope. "I am going to have another son," I cheered to myself as I walked out of the doctor's office, rubbing my growing baby belly. I could not have been happier.

Before leaving the parking lot, I began to call my family and friends to share the wonderful news. The news of a new son, whom we were naming Isaiah Christopher Ross. All of the calls were short and filled with congratulations for our family.

As I continued from weeks thirteen to nineteen, I would often feel a very sharp pain in the bottom of my uterus that would bring my body to an immediate halt. I would sit down for about twenty minutes and then slowly get up and continue with my daily activity. Continued ultrasounds would show new blood atop the old.

Overall, the doctor still seemed to stay positive and told me that as long as I felt good and my body stayed healthy, there was nothing to worry about. I kept a constant watch over how my body spoke to me from day to day. If I had a lot of abdominal pain during the day, I would allow myself frequent periods of rest. To the best of my ability, I tried to follow a strict daily routine.

Though I tried to be strong on a daily basis, fear of losing my son filled my thoughts. While gripped in fear, I tried to remind myself that our Lord is in control. I had to truly wrap my thoughts around this concept called *faith*. I often meditated on Hebrews 11:1, "Now faith is the substance of things hoped for, the evidence of things not seen." The word *faith* sounds so beautiful and gentle, but honestly, my refusal to believe what that ultrasound machine was showing me each month was emotionally exhausting. My job as a believer is to apply God's Word to my life. So I had to "walk the walk," if you will. I had to go into that doctor's office and keep smiling. I had to be brave for the onlookers, disbelievers, and the people silently crossing their fingers for me. I made a decision to walk with God. Even if that meant He would have to carry me through parts of the journey.

The journey of this pregnancy and numerous ultrasounds was quickly coming to an end. If only I had known that the days of his life were going to be shortly numbered, I would have begged to stay a little longer and watch my son dance on that black and white screen. I would have lain there as long as the doctor allowed, trying to figure out his personality. If only I had known that he would live longer in the warmth of my womb than in my arms, I would have memorized his every flip, kick, and wave of his hands. My prayers would have been desperate; I would have begged God to spare my little boy.

Just as Isaiah was being nurtured within my womb, I was being nurtured within the hands of the Lord. The Lord was preparing me for the path that lay ahead. When I needed peace, He would whisper to my soul, "I am peace." When I needed hope, He would whisper, "I am your hope."

At nineteen weeks pregnant, as I traveled down that darkened highway to the hospital, He held me under His wings ever so tightly and whispered, "Be not afraid."

"What time I am afraid, I will trust in thee" (Psalms 56:3).

I knew that the Lord held us both that night, but I was very afraid. Afraid that my motherly intuition was going to be correct. Afraid that this was the end for my son. Now was the time to cling to the substance of things hoped for. Faith, that beautiful and gentle word.

# Chapter 4

Inside that speeding ambulance, the darkness of night surrounded the team of paramedics and me. Though my eyes were shut, I was aware of the strobes of bright light. It felt as if I were in a dream. Only this time, I could only wish I were dreaming.

The ambulance sounded off with a high-pitched beep as it backed toward the side doors of the emergency room. The heavy doors of both the ambulance and hospital were swung open. Nurses began assisting the paramedics as the wind whipped through their thin scrubs. The stretcher that had securely locked me into place was carefully pulled out. The folded legs were quickly dropped. As the wheels met the pavement, my eyes opened just enough to have my gaze meet the gaze of my mother. A gust of wind blew through her hair as she approached. I found an immediate comfort in knowing that she was only an arm's length away. In the middle of her step, a nurse quickly directed her to the doors of the waiting room.

As I was wheeled down the hall, the fluorescent lights on the ceiling took turns shining upon the white blanket that covered my son and me. An empty room had been prepared and was waiting for my arrival. Gripping ever so tightly, the nurses pulled out the corners of the sheets that were tucked under the bed of the gurney and carefully placed me onto the hard ER bed. At this point, I couldn't function. I only remember hearing the nurses talk among themselves and ask me questions about what happened at home. I was answering, but no words were coming out. All you could hear was the sound of my teeth chattering.

I remember feeling completely desperate to receive the proper help. If I could have spoken, they would have heard me plead, "Get me up to the OB now!" All I wanted was a doctor who specialized in pregnancy and preterm labor. I needed to put a stop to the violent contractions. My child required many more weeks of being nurtured within my womb. Buying time became an urgent necessity.

The next thing I knew, a couple of nurses were transporting me to the OB floor. Maybe they could read the desperation on my face. The only sounds that could be heard were the hard black wheels rolling at a fast walking speed and my moans caused by the early contractions taking over my abdomen.

As the nurses prepared to turn the corner, they used all of their weight to stop the bed. I couldn't believe my eyes. Coming down the passing hall was another pregnant mother. What was the chance that we would come upon one another at the exact same time?

I can still see her in my mind as if it were yesterday. She had medium brown hair with a slight wave. Her smile was filled with excitement, knowing that she was only hours from delivering and meeting her child for the very first time. She held her baby belly with a mother's pride.

"Looks like you had better go first," one of her male nurses said with a chuckle to my nurse as he quickly stopped the bed of that glowing woman. Could they not tell that my cries of pain were not laced with happiness and joy for my unborn child? Did the size of my belly, compared with her full-term belly, not show the immediate medical help I required?

After a short ride up the elevator, we arrived in an area that I was familiar with. I had been in obstetrics three times prior to this pregnancy, with the joyful births of my three older boys. Even the smell brought with it sweet memories. I felt an immediate security.

I was rolled into a labor and delivery room. There, awaiting my arrival, were my husband and mother. The nurses gently placed me on a comfortable bed. Mom and Chris greeted me with words of comfort, and a nurse began an IV above my wrist so that my body could receive some much-needed fluids for the baby and myself. A urine sample had also been collected because an ER doctor thought I might have a urinary tract infection. To me, that sounded ridiculous, but I was in no condition to argue about my health.

My obstetrician had been notified of my admittance into the hospital, and she had requested that I be given a medication to help stop the contractions immediately. I was obliged to swallow those blessed pills as quickly as possible.

Remember, this was a race against time. Time that was absolutely essential for that little boy who innocently played within my womb. Who relied completely on all the choices that I would be making for his life and myself. His life was my priority.

As long as the contractions continued to dissipate, the doctor was going to check on me in the early morning. After the first hour, my contractions were slowing down. With each passing hour, I was relieved to experience fewer contractions. I was hopeful of having a full recovery following the unfortunate event of my preterm labor.

After my contractions slowed, my mom went home, believing that everything was going to be fine. For the rest of the night, my husband slept in a chair at my bedside as I tried to rest the best I could, catching a little sleep throughout the night. I was not only physically exhausted but also emotionally drained after all of the stress that my body had endured in those first couple of hours.

With all that was going on with me and my unborn son, my three older boys still occupied my thoughts. How are they going to react with their mother in the hospital? Are they going to cry and keep asking to come and see me? Or, will they simply let it appear to roll off their shoulders but instead hold their worries inside?

Oh, how I wish I could have been there to hold them. Better yet, I wish I could have been waking up in my own bed and making breakfast for them that morning. As I always say, it's better to pray then wish, and that's all I was doing that morning after waking up in my hospital bed.

Two new nurses checked in that morning for the day shift, and they came quietly into my room to introduce themselves. As I turned my head to meet them, I saw my cousin Misty. She was only a handful of months older than I was. We spent a lot of time together when we were little girls, and now she was going to be taking care of me. It was not only special to have her help, but it also brought me some childhood peace.

The other nurse gently checked my vitals and asked me how my night was. In a raspy voice, I told her that I felt weak but a lot better. She asked if I could get up and use the bathroom. That way we could see how I was doing physically and whether my contractions would start up again with the pressure of the baby pushing on my cervix.

It seemed to take a lot of effort to get myself into a sitting position. The nurse noticed I was struggling, and she helped pull my legs over the side of the bed and allowed me to use her arm so that I could stand to my feet. After standing at the side of my bed for a minute or two, I was able to get myself up and to the bathroom and back without any help, which was not only pleasing to me but also to the nurse. I returned to my bed and lay down. At that point, I thought maybe all I needed was lots of fluids and rest. Then, I could return home to my husband and children. I would have to be on bed rest until further notice, but at least I could be with my family, and my littlest boy would be able to continue his gymnastics, safely tucked away in my belly.

Just as these positive thoughts rushed happily through my mind, I felt something exit my body. My eyes locked with the eyes of the nurse. "Something just came out of me," I fearfully exclaimed. In the back of my mind, all I could picture was my son lying right on the sheet next to my warm body. I could tell from her body language that she feared the same.

The nurse quickly pulled the sheet back. "It's a blood clot," she confirmed. I could tell that she was as relieved as I was to hear this good report.

Come to find out, all of the contractions I was having the night before were associated with the delivery of this blood clot that we had been watching grow from the beginning of my pregnancy. The trouble-making blood clot was gone!

My doctor arrived shortly after the blood clot exited my body and did a thorough ultrasound. She pointed out the placenta and the area where the clot abrupted. It was still bleeding. The caution flag was raised, along with my worries for my son—again.

The doctor checked his heartbeat and watched for any fetal distress. Nothing. There was not one problem with that little boy. His heartbeat was strong. As strong as his swift kicks and somersaults. He was not going anywhere, and I was not giving up hope.

My doctor did not seem as happy as I did about the news. Then, after she began speaking, I realized why her enthusiasm was non-existent. She began to explain the bleed atop the placenta and the care that both my baby and I were going to require. Her concern was how the abruption had torn the placenta—the organ that was vital to keeping the baby healthy and alive. He not only received blood and nutrients from it but also oxygen. After she had finished explaining the medical issues that he and I were facing, she ended with these words: "He has a one percent chance at survival."

I still refused to believe.

My doctor wanted me to be transferred by ambulance to Spectrum Health in Grand Rapids, Michigan, three and a half hours away. That hospital had an up-to-date NICU where the doctors specialized specifically in the care of premature babies. I would be carefully monitored and cared for while awaiting my son's early arrival.

I was only nineteen weeks and three days pregnant. I needed to keep my pregnancy going at least up to the twenty-four week mark. As I mentioned earlier in the book, babies rarely are born at twenty-four weeks gestation without serious health problems. There is an increased risk of lasting disabilities, such as mental retardation, learning and behavioral problems, cerebral palsy, lung problems, and vision and hearing loss.

I was willing to do whatever I needed for my son, no matter what it required. I couldn't imagine being away from home for months, but I knew it would all be worth it. We would all get through this tough time and come out stronger in the end.

After I understood the risks that my pregnancy held, I agreed to be sent to Spectrum Health. My doctor ordered some blood labs to be conducted before my leaving. She wanted to check different levels in my blood not only to make sure that I was as healthy as possible before I was transferred but also to give the hospital an up-to-date record on my health. That way, the new doctors could compare my old numbers with any changes as I was monitored in their care.

Along with the main blood draw to check my general health, my doctor had a specific test called a D-dimer conducted. Due to the weeks I had been slowly bleeding and then the abruption from the placenta, she needed to take special precautions. A D-dimer test may be used as an aid in the assessment of thromboembolism. It would show the doctor how my body was dealing with the trauma of the abruption and continued bleed that was taking place on my placenta. My blood was drawn for these specific tests, and we patiently waited for the results.

While waiting for the results of the blood test, my husband and I had a few visitors. My sister, Ashlee, brought me some beautiful flowers and sat with me for a while. She encouraged me with happy thoughts of my son being born healthy and spent a lot of time trying to keep me smiling.

After my sister left the hospital, two pastors from our church visited with me and Chris. I told them that, earlier in the morning, the doctor had said that the baby had only a 1% chance at survival. I remember smiling at them and telling them about my oldest son, Caleb, "who just had a brain tumor removed a little over a year ago. God saved his life, and He is going to save this child's life too," I said with a confident smile. The pastors kept their visit short because they knew that I needed my rest. They prayed for our unborn child to be healthy and safe, and that God would give the doctor wisdom over the care that he and I would require for the remainder of my pregnancy.

Not long after our pastors had left my room, my doctor came back to check on me. Before she even said a word, a look of concern radiated off her like steam rolling off the top of a hot cup of coffee. She shook her head with regret and began to tell me that my blood labs were not good. She went on to explain that the D-dimer blood test was showing an elevation in the clotting factor within my blood to the degree of my body slowly bleeding to death. She called this Disseminated Intravascular Coagulation (DIC). DIC is a serious disorder in which the proteins that control clotting become abnormally active. Normally when you are injured, certain proteins in the blood become activated and travel to the injury site to help stop bleeding. However, in persons with DIC, these proteins become abnormally active. Small blood clots form in the blood vessels. Some of these clots can clog up the vessels and cut off blood supply to various organs, such as the liver, brain, or kidneys. These organs will then be damaged and may stop functioning.

After receiving this terrible news, my doctor continued with a sigh in every sentence. As she tried to hold back the tears, she said, "Jenny, we need to send new blood up to the lab and compare the new numbers with the old. If the numbers in your blood are showing an increase in clotting, we need to deliver."

I didn't know how to respond to that statement. I simply couldn't grasp the medical conflict that was going on inside my body or wrap my mind around the danger that I was facing. Before I could think of more questions for my doctor, the phlebotomist entered my room to take my blood. My doctor quietly exited.

I lay there in disbelief. At that point, I was ready to wake up from the nightmare. I could not believe that this was happening to me. This is the sort of drama you see on television and read about in books and magazines. I was not cut out for this kind of loss. Nor was I willing to give up a child whom I planned, carried within my womb, sang and talked to while rubbing my tummy, and loved with an unconditional love that cannot be put into words.

I could not fathom losing a child. Having three older boys, I knew exactly what I would be losing. My love ran to the innermost depths of my soul for my children. I would do anything for them. I would give my life to save theirs. As I lay there in that hospital bed, I was being told to do the opposite. My son may have to die so I can live!

In a matter of about twenty minutes, my doctor stepped into my room and sat at the end of my bed. She gently placed her hand on my leg and looked me straight in the eyes. My motherly intuition began processing her quiet walk into the room and the look in her eyes that spoke volumes. I knew it was over. My hopes. My dreams. His life.

"In my distress I called upon the Lord, and cried to my God: and he did hear my voice out of his temple, and my cry did enter into his ears" (2 Samuel 22:7).

It wasn't my voice that the Lord heard at that moment, but my heart. It was crying out from the depths of my soul, "Noooooo! No! Not my little boy!" My heart was pleading with God. "Please, God! Please don't allow this to happen!"

My doctor told me that I was dying and needed to be induced immediately. A look of despair covered my face, and my head slowly shook. No. I can't do this.

Not to God.

Not my family.

Not to my son.

# CHAPTER 5

"There *must* be something we can do," I said in a way that demanded a solution that would spare my child's life.

My doctor continued explaining that once the numbers rose too high, there was no turning them around. It was an all-around death sentence. I will never forget her next words: "You are going to die if we do not get the placenta out as soon as we possibly can. You are bleeding to death." Those were the words as plain as day.

She continued to plead with me. "We have to get that placenta out of you now. You only have a thirty percent chance at surviving the birth within the first twenty-four hours."

My mother and husband were in the room with me. They heard the terrifying words spoken by my doctor and were shocked speechless.

The doctor went on to tell me that I needed to get blood transfusions started too. I studied her eyes closely. She had known me for over seven years and had delivered my three older boys. I trusted her. Not only her knowledge with pregnancy and delivery but as a mother. She was a mother too, and I knew that she would not intentionally hurt an innocent child.

I requested to talk to the head guy in the NICU. He was working not far down the hallway. My request was granted, and he came to my room and answered all my questions. I asked what we could do to save the life of my son. He answered, "I have never seen a baby survive when born this young." He continued, "The baby may live for a short period of time . . . but will not live long." I was not going to find a solution from this guy, so I thanked him for answering my questions and let him return to his work in the NICU.

I was out of options. I had nowhere to turn, no one to wake me up. This was real life, and I needed to make a choice. I just did not know what to do. How could I allow my child to die? How could any mother or father allow their child to die? At that point, life had become inhumane. I simply said, "I cannot do this!"

What I heard next were words that continually echo through my mind. "It's one of you, or both of you." I lay there in shock. Fear began to take hold of me. No one was accepting any other options that I threw out there. This was serious. As every minute passed, I drew a little closer to death.

Within a few minutes of hearing the words "It's one of you, or both of you," I nodded in agreement for an induction. At that exact moment, I went against every belief I have ever clung to. I have never believed that it is acceptable for an individual to take a life. I believe in giving life. Who was I to take a life that my husband and I planned? A life that God created. The very life that the Lord formed in my womb, I was taking out. By agreeing to an early induction, I became a mother who had to step aside and allow harm to come upon my child. At that exact moment, I lost a piece of myself.

I had to sign papers to receive blood transfusions. As soon as I sat that pen down, my doctor looked over at the door of my room and nodded to the other nurses to get everything set up to begin the induction. Those nurses seemed to pour into the room. They literally had been standing outside my door with bags of blood packed in dry ice. I had to have another IV started in my other arm so I could get blood pumped into my body faster.

My cousin Misty sat next to me on my bed and simply said, "I'm going to cry." I just stared at the wall in disbelief.

My husband and mother left the room to start making phone calls to our family and friends. Not only to share the horrific news of the impending death of our son, but to ask for prayer regarding my health.

As they were making those calls, my cousin stepped to the head of my bed and handed me four little white pills. Called Cytotec, those pills would start my uterus contracting so that my cervix would open up enough to allow the birth of my son and, of course, the placenta. I held those little white pills in the palm of my hand and closed my eyes. I gently placed my other hand on my violet maternity shirt that, to this day, I don't know why I still wore instead of a hospital gown. Maybe it was simply so I could have a special moment with my son, just as I had done minutes before having to call 9-1-1 the night before.

Twenty-four hours hadn't even passed, and I was embracing every flip, kick, and hiccup for the last time. I felt my baby's joy and love as he danced under my hand. Sorrow washed over me, knowing that my womb would protect him for only a few more hours. Just as I had wondered if he could feel my fear as I was taken in the ambulance the night before, I lay there and wondered if he could feel my sadness. This was the last of my pregnancy.

I brought my hand to my mouth and paused. This was plain torture. Instead of swallowing a prenatal vitamin for health benefits, I had to put this poison in my body. I placed the pills in my mouth and could not swallow. I felt a few more kicks and flips, placed them deep in my memory to hang onto, and then swallowed.

About five minutes later, I was given Pitocin through my IV, another medication to help start labor. I knew that in about an hour tops, I would be having painful contractions, but there was no way that my physical pain would come close to touching the pain that my soul was being subjected to.

# Chapter 6

I screamed out in pain, "I can't do this to him! I love him so much!" A cloud of sorrow accompanied my words as they pierced through the hearts of all who could hear my anguish.

Rita, the youth pastor's wife from my church, was working that night at the hospital. She was a nurse in the ICU. She had heard about my admittance into the hospital and came to the OB department to check on me. She stayed in my room for a little while, trying to comfort me. She stood at my bedside, massaging my back through violent rounds of contractions. It was comforting to know that a woman of faith was aware of what was happening. I trusted her to speak up against the induction, if need be. Unfortunately, that was not to be. She was only able to visit for a short time before she had to return to the ICU.

Darkness grew outside my window, and one of the nurses closed the drapes. It was getting closer to the end. The end of me protecting that little boy's life. My body continued to supply him blood, nutrients, and oxygen as it depleted me from all the essential elements that it took for me to stay alive and healthy. With each second ticking away on the clock, my son and I came closer to exchanging health conditions.

I felt as though my insides were being torn to pieces. The impending death was approaching.

With limited time to spare, I took it all in. I closed my eyes and gently placed my hand on my belly. Our souls connected. It was as though he knew that I wanted to spend the last moments together "alone." He gave me some gentle kicks and elbow nudges, showing off for his proud mommy just as he had the night prior as I lay resting in my bed.

This was my last opportunity to interact with my son. The last time I would feel him full of life. The last moments of his life. I could protect him no longer. I cried out in pain, "I have to push!"

A group of nurses and my doctor rushed to my bedside. My doctor sat at the end of my bed and checked me. Consumed with sadness, she softly said, "It's time."

She could see the baby's head and told me to take a deep breath and push. A few more pushes, and Isaiah Christopher Ross was born into this cold world out of my warm, nurturing womb on August 3, 2008, at 8:45 p.m. There was no more safety for this innocent boy.

My doctor quickly looked him over to see if he was farther along in gestation so that his life could be saved; however, the charts and ultrasound predictions had been correct. He was nineteen weeks and three days along. There was no way to keep him alive.

The nurse placed her stethoscope over his heart to check for a heartbeat. It was still beating. He was a strong little boy. A fighter for his own life.

With my husband off in the distance with intense emotion overtaking every cell in his body, my mom near my bedside, and nurses giving me personal space, my baby was carefully placed in my arms. I was in complete awe of how beautiful that little boy was. For a moment, the world felt "right." Time stopped, and the knowledge that he would soon be gone was forgotten.

He was completely formed. Ten fingers. Ten toes. A tiny boy, too weak to live on his own. I put my thumb in the palm of his left hand and gently rubbed his smooth skin. I leaned forward and whispered, "Mommy loves you, Isaiah Christopher Ross." I whispered it repeatedly. I wanted him to hear my voice. To know that I was right there with him.

The nurse checked for a heartbeat again. She affirmed with a nod that he was still alive. My motherly instincts were running full force as I asked for another blanket to keep him warm. My request was quickly attended to, and a nurse helped me tuck the blanket around him. I rubbed the side of my thumb along his delicate, chubby baby cheek to bring about a calmness to his mind, body, and soul.

A loud beep went off on a machine that stood near the backside of my bed. Isaiah lifted his right arm. I believe that because the noise was so loud, it had startled him. That noise was a gift to me. I saw life. I saw my son move, for the first time . . . and the last.

Isaiah's heartbeat was checked again by the nurse. She gently let me know that his heart was drastically slowing and asked if I wanted him to be baptized. I needed no time to think on that question. I immediately said yes. She walked over to the counter to retrieve the oil. Every person in that room came over to my bed where I held that precious boy and closed their eyes. The oil was gently massaged on his tiny head, and the baptism proceeded. When his baptism was finished, his heartbeat was checked again. I was told that he had only a few minutes left.

How was I to fill his last minutes? I had a lifetime of things I wanted to say and do with that little boy. I did all that I knew to do. Cradling him closer to my chest, I told him how proud I was to be his mommy. I told him how strong and brave he was as I held his hand in mine. The whispers of "I love you, Isaiah" were many.

After holding him for a few minutes, his heartbeat was checked again. He was gone. Isaiah was delivered into the arms of his Heavenly Father at 9:00 p.m. In that moment, I felt a piece of my own heart stop beating.

I was given fifteen minutes to speak a lifetime of "I love you's" into his ear. Fifteen minutes to hold his hand. The hand that would have given me countless "high fives" had he lived.

A little life that would have been, but isn't.

# Chapter 7

With a farewell kiss toward heaven, I gently handed my son over to a waiting nurse. We still had not accomplished the reason behind my induction. I was bleeding heavily and needed to deliver the placenta.

"Give me a good hard push, Jenny," my doctor said authoritatively. With all my might, I pushed. Nothing. "Push again, Jenny. Put your chin to your chest and give me all you have," the doctor directed again. Nothing.

Through the dimmed lighting, I could see my doctor's concern. It was written all over her face. "Jenny, we have to get the placenta out now," she said in a low voice with a bit of fear trickling off her words.

I was pushing as hard as I could. With every ounce of strength that I had left, I pushed one more time. As I pushed, my doctor tried to pull out the placenta. A nurse was holding my arms down, trying to help calm me. I gasped in the middle of my push and let out a scream that must have echoed through the halls of the OB department. The doctor quickly removed her hand. My body seemed to deflate from the top of my head to the ends of my toes, just like a balloon with a leak.

I was exhausted. I wanted no more of this. With a whisper, the following words passed over my dry, almost lifeless lips: "I'm done. I can't do anymore. Put me out." I had nothing left to give. I had given my all, my son. All I wanted was to avoid feeling anything else. No pain. No sadness. Just to go numb, under a general anesthesia.

Just as the ER doctor and nurses seemed to have read the desperation in my face to get the proper help for my unborn son, my doctor could read the agony written deep within my eyes. She ordered the operating room to be set up immediately.

In a swift manner, my bed was rolled down to the OR. While waiting for the anesthesiologist, my jaw began to shake, and my teeth started chattering. Then my body followed the leading of my jaw, and I began to shake uncontrollably. I could feel myself dying. For once, I had an understanding of how someone could want to give up. To let go. To die.

A clear mask was placed over my nose and mouth, and I began to inhale the mixture of gases. With a surgical mask covering his mouth and only his eyes visible, I made a silent connection with the anesthesiologist. Looking deep into his eyes, our souls met, and I thanked him with a long exhale, as sleep fell upon me.

A D&C (dilation and curettage) was performed after I drifted into a deep sleep. It had taken my doctor an hour and a half to perform a ten-minute job. I received many blood transfusions during that time. Surgical sponges were put in my uterus every few minutes to help stop the bleeding. After the sponges were removed, my doctor would continue to remove pieces of placenta. Some were as small as the tips of her fingers. As she continued packing sponges and removing pieces, she came across part of the placenta that had grown into my uterus. That was the reason I was unable to deliver the placenta. A placenta accreta is a severe obstetric complication involving an abnormally deep attachment of the placenta through the endometrium and into the myometrium (the middle layer of the uterine wall).

The placenta usually detaches from the uterine wall relatively easily, but women who encounter placenta accreta during childbirth are at great risk of hemorrhage during its removal. This commonly requires surgery to stem the bleeding and fully remove the placenta, and in severe forms can often lead to a hysterectomy or death.

I was on the borderline of needing a hysterectomy, but my well-educated doctor continued to do all that she could. Her priority was my health, and performing surgery carried with it the great possibility of killing me, not to mention leaving me with more loss to wake up to if I survived.

As all of my medical needs were being attended to, I like to believe that God gave me some special time with my son. Because Isaiah's death was so fresh and I was so close to death, I like to imagine the love of my son wrapping around me, whispering that he was right there with me, just as I had whispered to him as he lay dying in my arms. Maybe that is what got me through.

The surgery was finished, my vitals were checked one last time before leaving the OR table, and I was wheeled to the ICU. I remained there through the night, heavily sedated, drifting in and out of consciousness. At one point, I awoke to a nurse standing next to my bed, asking me if I wanted to hold Isaiah. What? In a matter of seconds, it all came flooding back. I had flashbacks of Isaiah dancing in my belly, having him placed in my arms for the first time, the nurse nodding her head to confirm that the beating of his heart had come to an end, and the heart-throbbing torture of handing him over to the nurse after cradling him for only fifteen minutes. I immediately called my mother and started to cry and speak incoherently. She asked me to slow down and tell her what was going on. I blurted out, "A nurse is in my room asking me if I want to hold Isaiah. I don't know what to do!"

I could hear the panic in Mom's voice as she consoled me, telling me to do what my heart wanted. I spoke a simple "okay" and hung up the phone. I was alone and terrified beyond words. I told the nurse that I did not know what to do, and she assured me that I need not make any decisions at that moment. She had asked me if I wanted him to be taken to the morgue because it might be a while before I made up my mind. I agreed to that plan. To this very day, I have not gotten over the fact that I gave that nurse permission to place my son in a cold, dark morgue! Saying the words makes me sick, as does thinking about it in general. I have to allow myself a "freebie," as I did not have any prior experience with death and the decisions one must make after the death of a loved one.

I slept through the rest of the night with brief wakes from nurses who continued to check my vitals and make sure that the bleeding in my uterus was normal. Monitoring my blood flow to ensure that no signs of hemorrhage were appearing.

As the light of dawn began to creep between the cracks of my drapes, I slowly returned to my living nightmare. The anesthesia had worn off, and I was fully coherent. My eyes would open slightly and then close. I was physically, mentally, and emotionally exhausted. I looked at a clock that was mounted to the wall in front of my bed. It was almost 6:45 a.m. As my eyes were closing, I caught a glimpse of a man standing at my doorway. It was a minister. With a gentle smile, he said a soft hello. This man had to be in his late fifties and was clean-shaven with gray streaks of hair outlining the black. "I hear that you lost your son last night, and I was wondering if I could pray with you," he said, keeping his voice to a quiet monotone. I nodded my head in agreement. The minister began praying. His voice was very soothing but, to be honest, I do not remember one word. I remember feeling numb. I was aware of life around me, but I do not think that I was ready to wake up and face the events that had unfolded hours earlier. The prayer was finished, and the man looked at me and then at the floor. My eyes closed again. Hesitating at my bedside, he softly assured me, "If you need to talk or would like more prayer, just let your nurse know, and I will be happy to visit with you again." I nodded and thanked him as my voice cracked.

Right after the minister left, my stepfather, Keith, came into my room. He had been at the hospital the night prior, praying and pacing the floor of the waiting room. He smiled as he approached my bedside, but I could see the sorrow in his eyes. With an encouraging voice, he said, "I saw a rainbow over the bay as I was driving here. It was beautiful." If I had had the strength at the time, I would have pulled myself off that hard hospital bed to tiptoe over to my window and peer out over the horizon. I couldn't move, but I could see the beauty of that rainbow through Keith's smile. His face seemed to have captured every color that had radiated off the arch of God's handiwork.

Before leaving, Keith carefully leaned over and planted a gentle kiss on my forehead. In that one kiss, I could feel the thankfulness he had to God for allowing me to live. A thanksgiving for his answered prayers. As he headed toward the door to go to work, he turned around and said, "I love you." Without speaking, I allowed myself to give half a smile. *I know, Keith, I know*, I thought to myself as I watched him walk out the door.

I had to face facts: my son died. I knew that this was the first step of my journey.

Picking up the phone that was hanging on the rail of my bed, I began to dial my father's cell phone number. He and my stepmother, Jen, were on a road trip vacation at the time. This would be the first time that I heard my dad's voice in days. I never had gotten the chance to speak to him after arriving at the hospital. He had been continually updated with my health crisis via phone from different family members. After the second ring, I heard a soft "hello." He knew it was me. In that very second, our hearts connected. I felt as though he were standing in my room, right next to my bed, holding my hand. With all the strength that I could gather in my brokenness, I softly breathed the words, "I lost him, Dad. He died." I closed my eyes as they filled with tears.

The next sound I heard over the quietness in that phone line was an emotion that ran deep within my dad's soul. He began to weep. I have never heard a pain so deep exit that man's soul. With his voice trembling, he began to tell me what he was witnessing at that very moment. "Jenny, I'm looking out over the ocean right now, and there is one of the most beautiful double rainbows I have ever seen."

In that instant, I knew that I was receiving a priceless gift from God. One of hope, love, and peace. We ended the phone call with emotional "I love you's" and said goodbye.

After gathering my wits, I made one last phone call—to my friend Phyllis. To be completely honest, Phyllis is my ex-mother-in-law, but I prefer to call her my friend. We have remained close following the divorce of her son and I. Whenever I needed immediate help with Caleb, she was always there for me, day or night. I needed to inform her of the fragility of my health and—more importantly—the loss of Isaiah. As soon as the words left my lips, she began sobbing. I couldn't understand her words, but I knew that she was in disbelief. For me. For Isaiah. She has always loved me as if I were her own daughter. I could feel the love mixed with heartbreaking pain as her words traveled into my ear.

I caught a word among the mess of tears. The word *rainbow*. "I'm standing here looking out my bay window right now, and in the distance, right over the lake, there is a beautiful rainbow in the sky." Her crying intensified. "I have never seen colors this bright in a rainbow, Jenny!" In that short period of time, I was physically and emotionally worn. "I am so sorry, Jen. I am so sorry," she repeated as we ended our phone call.

Lying in my bed with my eyes shut, I mentally wrapped the special gift of the rainbows from God and tucked it away, deep in my heart. Three phone calls, each containing a rainbow, all in a half-hour time frame. This was not a coincidence.

Each rainbow had appeared over a body of water. I found comfort in thinking that the water represented the many tears that would travel over my cheeks throughout the years to come, mixed with the unending love and hope that God gives.

As I lay resting on my bed, guilt began to fill my conscience. My son died so that I could live! There are no words to describe the emotional pain that consumed my aching heart.

I closed my eyes and began to pray. I needed comfort drenched with love from my Heavenly Father. I climbed into His mighty arms, whispering my thoughts, as He cradled me just as He had done with my son hours earlier.

# Chapter 8

My back ached as I tried to sit up in my bed after being moved into a private room. Placed on the opposite side of the steel doors separating obstetrics and pediatrics, I was enveloped in complete silence. No cries of newborn life could be heard there. All that surrounded me was a pattern of blue boats outlining the four walls within my room.

Weakness overtook my body, and once more, I drifted in and out of consciousness. Family and friends brought me flowers and heartfelt condolences as they encompassed me with their love. When they spoke to me, I could see their pain as I gazed deep within their eyes, their souls. They knew as well as I that I wasn't "out of the woods" yet, that my health was slowly improving but was still lacking much-needed strength. My eyes closed as small talk continued. All I could think about was that little boy as I continued to have flashbacks of the purity and innocence evident upon his face and felt along each tiny finger.

One of the hardest moments was approaching: the deliverance speech to my older boys, telling them that their much-anticipated brother was no longer living. I did not know what to say or how to say it. The dreams of a child are much different from those of an adult. In a child's mind, no harm can happen. Invincibility is the power they hold. Not this day. Their superhero capes were going to need to be hung up at the doorway.

My sons were not aware that their brother had been born. They just knew that I had gotten really sick in the night. I wanted to be the first to tell them, to answer their questions. The answers would be the very thing that would change their lives forever on this earth.

My mom and stepfather came up to my room and counseled me on the safest way to present the loss of their brother to the boys. After we came up with a plan, I contacted my friend Jen, who had been tending to the care of my boys, and asked her to bring them to the hospital so I could see and speak to them.

Mom and I were talking when I heard the patter of feet nearing my room. My heart seemed to stop, knowing that my sons' world was going to come crashing down. They peeked around the door, giving me half smiles. Jen and her daughter Alexis waited out in the hallway.

It was so refreshing to see those three precious faces. I wanted nothing more than to have them lie on my bed with me so I could hold them close, feeling their little bodies and soft skin, smelling the "boy" all over them. I needed my boys.

They shuffled to the right of my bed. The boys saw that I must have delivered when they noticed that my belly was no longer round with child. With eager smiles and pure excitement—but still keeping their voices low in case the baby was sleeping—they asked to see their new brother.

I could not speak.

With concern in their voices and a tilt of their heads, they asked, "Where is he, Mom?"

My lips parted slightly, and I whispered, "He's with Jesus." All of our eyes filled with tears in that moment.

They could not speak.

I looked at my mom through my tear-filled, clouded vision, silently seeking her guidance. She suggested letting the boys take turns being alone with me. Then, each one could have time to ask me questions regarding the loss. Because they were ages three, five, and seven, their individual questions would be different on so many levels.

After speaking to each boy alone, a sense of shock was clearly visible on each face. I felt so helpless. A sugar cookie or new Hot Wheels toy car would not fix the disappointment and pain that filled the hearts of these boys. They stayed with me for a short time, and then I gave them each a hug and kiss before they left to go home. Every fiber of my being wanted to pack my personal items and take my sons home myself. Overcome with sadness, I watched them walk out the door with grief weighing down their young shoulders. Again, my heart seemed to stop as I listened to their footsteps softly travel down the hallway, away from my room.

My mom approached and gently rubbed my leg, assuring me that I had done a good job of telling the boys about the loss of Isaiah. They would be okay. I nodded as I let out an emotional sigh. Mom comforted me with a mother's intuitive love and, shortly after, she and my stepfather took off for home. We all had expended every drop of energy we had.

With my husband out for a short bit, and my mom, stepfather, and boys returning home, I was left alone with that pattern of blue boats outlining the four walls within my room. Pain consumed my aching back and my shattered heart.

# Chapter 9

I searched my room with heavy, half-opened eyes for the gentle voice that repeated my name. It was my new nurse, who was overseeing my care for the day. I had a hard night trying to rest and recover following the difficult task of telling my boys that their little brother had passed.

I don't remember her name, but she had a peaceful spirit about her, and I felt as though she truly cared about my severed heart. She stood next to my bedside and simply asked if I wanted her to go get my little boy so that I could hold him.

The world stopped rotating on its axis! Immediately, I responded with confusion and excitement. "What?" Bewildered, I asked, "How can I see him? He has been in the morgue!" I looked down at the blanket that covered my legs, almost feeling ashamed that I would, and could, hold my child after he had been placed in a cold, dark, somewhat frightening place.

In a reassuring voice, she said, "Yes, you can hold him!" I quickly looked back up at her.

"What's he going to look like? I'm scared." As I awaited my answer, my mother-in-law, Judy, entered my room with some homemade food and a devotional book. She pulled up a chair and sat on the other side of my bed, opposite of the nurse. I turned to her and told her that my nurse had just informed me that she could go get Isaiah if I wanted to hold him. The look on her face revealed that she knew she had shown up at the right time. She would be able to meet her grandson. My voice shook as I looked back at my nurse and told her that I would like to hold him. She smiled and said, "I'll be right back with your son."

Could this really be happening? Am I really going to "get back" the precious jewel that I had lost only a little over twenty-four hours ago?

The nurse tiptoed into my room, ever so carefully cradling my baby, my son. A feeling of completeness washed over my soul. She leaned over, placing him in my empty arms, making them full again. "Let me know if there's anything else I can do for you," she said as she trailed out of the room.

Though he was lying in my arms dead, I still felt a sense of life. I really can't explain it. Maybe, it was because he was where he was supposed to be—in my arms.

Judy encouraged me to unwrap the pastel blanket that was swaddling his tiny body. I took one corner of the blanket in my hand, and then I hesitated. Fear took hold of me. "It's okay, Jenny," she whispered. In that very moment, adrenaline rushed through my veins. I unwrapped the blankets, revealing my precious son. Sobs broke loose from deep inside both our chests. I was crying so hard that I could not open my eyes, and when I finally was able, my vision was filled with the most beautiful sight I had ever seen. I was viewing a masterpiece created by the hands of God.

Isaiah had ten long fingers and ten cute little toes that each held a unique fingerprint that God designed just for him and him alone. Let me not forget to mention the tiny nails that made each finger and toe complete. His eyes were closed as if he were merely asleep, outlined with eyelashes that were as beautiful as the wings of angels. A cute button nose. Lips as red and soft as rose petals. Two ears that had heard the whispers of his mommy's endless "I love you's." He was as real as they come. A precious boy, fully developed. I was in a state of awe. Judy and I took it all in.

After I had held him for a while, the nurse came back to check on me. Judy got up to leave. I could tell that she was worn out, as her emotions wavered between grief and happiness. We shared some special time together and would always remember the moments that we "oohed and aahed" over Isaiah, sharing a little piece of heaven. That has been, by far, my greatest memory with my mother-in-law.

The nurse walked out with Judy, and I had my baby all to myself. I held in my arms a hero. I gently rubbed my thumb along his cheeks, knowing that the very life that I was holding was taken to save my own. A mother is the one known for giving the gift of life, but this time, it went the other way.

I cradled him, unwrapping his blankets again. I slowly searched his body, making a mental note of every piece that God had formed. I did not want to forget how he looked, how his soft skin felt, and who he was. This was my one day with him before handing him over forever.

I caressed his soft little legs. The very legs that would never ride a bike, play on a playground, or go for walks with me on a beautiful summer evening. I rubbed his little feet and counted each little toe. The very feet that would never be tickled by his mommy or daddy. The very toes that would never get to feel hot sand on a beach. I held his hands in mine, knowing that I would never get to hold them to play pat-a-cake, cross the road, or give high fives. I ran my hand over his smooth arms, knowing that he would never wrap them around my waist in a hug. I searched every feature on his face. He had the tiniest eyelashes—blondish red like his daddy's. The cutest button nose. As I looked at his smooth little lips, I realized that I would never get a kiss or hear an "I love you" spoken.

When I looked at his delicate ears, I had a deep peace, knowing that he had heard me tell him how much I loved him until the very last beat of his heart.

He was beautiful. Perfect. A priceless gift from God.

I cradled him tight within my arms, trying my hardest to capture that moment in my memory bank. I closed my eyes and rested for a little while.

Later that afternoon, two of my girlfriends, Tammy and Jodi, came to visit me, and they too held Isaiah. They were left breathless as they peeked at his tiny face. Tears of awe filled their eyes, seeing how precious he truly was.

While they took turns holding and rocking him, my nurse came to my room again. She asked me if I would like her to take some pictures of me holding Isaiah. As tears filled my eyes, I whispered "yes."

My sweet friend Tammy offered to brush my hair to somewhat help prep me for this once-in-a-lifetime photo. As she brushed through all the tangles and snarls that were left in my hair from labor and delivery, I watched Jodi rock my son as she hummed him a lullaby.

After I was prepared for my picture, Jodi placed Isaiah in my arms. She said, "You need to rock him too, Jenny." I silently rocked him, looking at his face and kissing the top of his head.

The next thing I knew, I was back in bed, having my picture taken as I cradled Isaiah close to my heart.

Shortly after our photos were taken, Tammy and Jodi took off to their own families, and Mom and Keith stopped by for one last visit with Isaiah, taking turns holding and talking to him. I watched from afar, capturing the image of Isaiah's grandparents loving on him as they said their final goodbyes. My mom then placed him in my arms, kissed the top of his head, and softly whispered, "I love you, Isaiah."

After giving me a hug and kiss, Mom and Keith left for home. I have never seen them so broken as I did in that moment.

Night came upon me, and darkness filled my room. Time had become my enemy. There were not many hours left for me to hold my son. I drifted off as he lay in my arms, as if we were at home.

He was mine, and yet he was God's.

# Chapter 10

My husband had gone back to our house to gather some clothes for me to wear for the drive home once I was released from the hospital. I was alone when a soft knock echoed off the door to my room. It was too soon for Chris to have returned. "Come in," I called softly, fearing that I knew who it was.

The door opened, and a man dressed in a sharp-looking black suit stepped in. My heart sank. This was the end.

The gentleman talked to me and answered all my questions. I tried to come up with as many as I could possible think of because I was not ready to hand my son over to the funeral director.

Isaiah had been taken to a room in the NICU earlier that morning. The nurse took him down there so that I could gather my thoughts and prepare for what I was about to face.

The funeral director walked with me to the NICU. I was looking at the same cream-colored walls, shadowed hallway, and fluorescent lights that I had traveled two days earlier with my son nestled safely within my womb. Now he lay swaddled in blankets, awaiting a final kiss from his mommy.

The nurse greeted us at the door with a peaceful smile, welcomed us in, and directed us toward the room where I was to go and say goodbye. I asked to be alone with my baby. They kindly granted my wish and left the door slightly cracked.

I stood there in my hospital slippers, feeling the cold from the hard floor penetrate through the fabric. I laid my hand upon his little body and tried to capture a mental picture of the precious face of my son. Every feature that God had perfectly sculpted was given to me for a short time, and now it was time to say goodbye.

How do you walk away from your child when all that has pieced you together for the last seven years of being a mother was to provide for and protect your children?

Would you ever take your child to a store, push that little boy or girl around in a shopping cart for a while, and then walk out the door to get in your vehicle and drive away, leaving that child behind? No! How could you? As a parent, you have a built-in protection shield for your children.

That morning, I didn't get to use my protection shield. Instead, I had to surrender this child of mine to be put in a box and taken to a funeral home.

I closed my eyes as I gently ran my finger down his smooth baby cheek. I kissed his little head, put my lips close to his ear, and whispered, "I love you, Isaiah Christopher Ross."

I turned to leave. My feet felt glued to the tiles. I turned back again, returning to where he lay. I rubbed his head, softly whispering how much I loved him. I told him how proud I was to be his mommy and that he would never be forgotten.

Never.

With a final kiss upon his head, I turned and walked out the door. I did not say one word to the nurse; I could not look the funeral director in the eyes. I headed for my room, looking at my feet as I trod those cold tiles. I felt pieces of me break away as I traveled back to my room. These were the beginning steps of my journey through life without Isaiah.

After returning to my room, I changed into some clothes that my husband had brought me from home. Shortly after changing and packing up my belongings, I signed paperwork to be discharged from the hospital.

As I was wheeled down the hallway, my husband and I crossed paths with one of our pastors from church. He was actually there to visit and pray with us before we left for home. He walked with us as my nurse pushed me along in a wheelchair. Once we reached the double sliding doors, I sat in the wheelchair and waited for Chris to get the van and pull it up.

I was escorted to the empty passenger seat. The air was warm, the sun was shining, and all I wanted to do was get on my knees and scream at the top of my lungs, "My son is dead!"

I held onto my composure as my husband helped me into our van. While he packed the van with flowers, plants, and personal items, I stared off into the sky, watching birds fly with the canvas of a blue sky behind them. Heaven was so close and yet so far away.

My husband and I didn't say a word to one another as we pulled away from the hospital. We marinated in the extreme emptiness that was left behind our own seats. With no baby to fill a car seat.

I sat in my seat with a swollen belly, empty arms, and a shattered heart. I have never felt so broken in my entire life, but at the same time, I never felt so close to the Lord. He held me as he had cradled Isaiah. If my faith were ever to be tested, the time was now. I didn't have answers, and yet, I still trusted.

# Chapter 11

The days seemed to melt away as I awaited the burial of my son. I had never before experienced a death so close to my own life, and now I needed to plan a heartfelt funeral and burial for a son whom I had not been able to play with, sing to, or even raise like my other boys. I had received a brief lesson in thorough love, learning how to completely and selflessly love another human—that being my son—in fifteen minutes of life on this earth. Sure, I had been able to rub my belly and sing/talk to him when he was dancing within my womb, but to love with the warmth of a child in your arms, caressing that soft baby skin and seeing that child look back into your eyes . . . nothing can top that. You feel complete in those moments.

After having to walk away from Isaiah at the hospital after telling him goodbye, I had to find enough courage and strength within myself to walk away from him again ... only this time it would be as I watched him being lowered in a cold dark hole that would somewhat swaddle him instead of the arms of his mommy. The strength that I could muster was from God alone. I was completely empty and numb. There are no classes during your pregnancy on how to care for a child who may pass away. That's the farthest thing from your mind. Your days are filled with daydreams for your little one. Days of changing diapers, feedings, and most of all, loving every little piece of that baby with every part of your being.

Rocking back and forth in my rocking chair as I sat in my darkened living room, I shuffled through every CD that I owned. It was the middle of the night. My husband and children were sleeping soundly, and I was in search of songs for Isaiah's funeral. I had to find songs that reflected my faith and trust in the Lord, the hope that I clung to, and the deep love that had been welded within my heart, mind, and soul for my son. I played various CDs until I found three songs that I wanted to play in honor of Isaiah:

"With Hope" by Steven Curtis Chapman

"Come to Jesus" from Power Lab VBS Untitled Hymn (originally by Chris Rice)

"Uncreated One" by Chris Tomlin

I felt satisfied with these choices. I climbed into bed, listened to my broken heart slowly beat, and drifted off to sleep.

On August 8, 2008, morning dawned quickly. I squinted at my alarm clock. I wasn't ready for this day, nor did I want to say good-bye again. I peeled my body from the sheets and got ready for the day, hoping for enough strength to make it to the afternoon. The kids ran around our home as if it were just another day. How I wished that I could turn back the clock to the days before I knew what loss felt like and simply enjoy the simplicity of a "normal" life. Normal would never be a feeling that would be in my grasp again. I awoke to a new life, one that would need to be learned from here on out.

A knock sounded at the door. It was my dad and stepmom, Jen. They had returned from their vacation just in time to bury their grandson. During an early-morning phone call, I had asked if they could pick up the boys some white shirts and black slacks to wear to their brother's burial and funeral. My dad handed me the packages holding their individual outfits, and emotion poured over me. I was filled with sorrow and anger all at the same time. It seemed as though each hour took me on a roller coaster ride of emotions.

I got the boys ready to pay their respects to their little brother. Daddy was soon ready too, looking sharp in his white dress shirt and black slacks.

Next, it was my turn. I stood at my closet, reaching in and pulling out a beautiful black and white dress. I undressed and carefully pulled the dress over my head, slid my arms through the sleeves, and let it fall into place. I looked in the mirror to see how I looked, and I immediately felt ill. Looking at the way the dress draped over my swollen, empty belly made me wonder if someone had played a sick joke on me. Not that it was possible to pull such a prank, but my mind was worn from stress. All I could think in that moment was *Is this really happening?*

I took the miniature Bible—specifically bought for Isaiah—that lay on my dresser and placed within it a photo of me cradling him in my arms. I placed it on Nahum 1:7. "The Lord is good, a strong hold in the day of trouble; and he knoweth them that trust in him." This I had to do: trust in the One who safely held my son, who held me. I placed a kiss on his sweet face and closed the Bible. That kiss would rest with Isaiah in the depths of the earth where I could not be.

Next, I took six white roses out of the dozen I had received at the hospital. Those six roses would rest on his casket, buried where I could not reach. White roses represent innocence and purity; they are a symbol of honor and reverence and are often used as an expression of remembrance. I could not have picked a better flower to represent that brave little boy.

After everyone had finished getting ready, we all got into our van, buckled up, and sat in complete silence. Chris drove us slowly to the cemetery. I took every mile in. Focusing on all that I was burying. Not only my son but also every single hope and dream I had for him as he grew within my womb.

When we pulled in, we had to follow many different signs directing us to the grave that would soon be Isaiah's. I tried to memorize every turn as we drove so I wouldn't forget how to get to his final resting place.

I spotted the black vehicle from the funeral home. My heart skipped, and my chest grew tight. We drove closer, and my eyes met that tiny white casket resting on top of a little bench. There he was, sealed away. Untouchable. God held me as I stepped out of the van.

Each step felt like an eternity as my heels sank into the damp dirt. I approached my pastor, Gary Mindel, and his wife, Lisakay. They were standing with the funeral director. They greeted us with gentle smiles. Honestly, I don't know whether I returned a smile. I had never felt so empty and helpless in my life. I stared at that casket. I wanted to pick it up and leave. My mind couldn't handle the thought of having dirt thrown over him. Tears welled up in my eyes.

As the minutes passed, close family members arrived to pay their respects. After all had arrived, Pastor Gary began with a prayer as a cool breeze blew through our hair and through the branches of the trees around us. Though it was a devastating event for me, it was beautiful as well. The sun's warmth fell upon our skin as if the Lord was breathing peace over us. Pastor Gary spoke with a perfect message of hope, love, and peace. I was pleased with his message and thankful that it was he who spoke in honor of my son. We closed in prayer, hugs, and a sincere thank you for his time. He and his wife left soon afterwards.

As I stood there, still gazing at Isaiah's casket, my brother Patrick put his hand on my shoulder and said, "It's going to be all right." That was a special moment to me. Two years apart in age, we grew up the best of friends. I have always felt very connected to him.

Then, my sister Ashlee hugged me, telling me how sorry she was that I had to go through such a heartbreaking experience. Pain and sorrow were etched on her face.

I stood silently as my mom and Keith took turns embracing me with hugs. They told me that they loved me and to call if I needed anything. After they glanced over at Isaiah's casket one more time, they left for home.

Next, my mother-in-law, Judy, placed a beautiful bracelet that she had made on my wrist. The sunlight reflected off the beads as if beaming with hope.

The last to come forward was my dad. He hugged me and then opened up my hand to place a flower bud in my palm as he spoke the words, "Started on earth as a bud, taken to heaven to bloom." I clung tightly to that bud as Dad gave me one last hug and left.

After everyone else had gone, Chris took the boys to the van, giving me a moment alone. I just stood there. My feet felt rooted to the ground. After I called up enough strength, I slowly walked toward that little white casket. I knelt down and gently rubbed the top. Then I gave it a gentle kiss. I knew that my kiss would be on it with Isaiah in that hole—my love for him would be buried with him. Though I knew that he was not really there but was instead experiencing the joys of heaven, this gesture gave me comfort.

I told the funeral director that I wanted to be present when he placed Isaiah below the earth. I had to make sure that he was placed with respect and gentleness. The funeral director respected my wishes and gently placed Isaiah to rest. He then took the Bible and placed it on top of the little white casket. Then I handed him the six white roses to be placed on top of the Bible. I wouldn't leave until I knew that everything was perfect, which it was, and so I didn't have any other reason to stay. There was nothing left to do. I had to walk away. I felt so empty. So angry. So sad. I had to leave behind a little boy that I never had an opportunity to do anything with. It was tragic!

My final act was to thank the funeral director for all of the support had given me. Then, breathing in the scent of wet dirt and carrying the weight of sorrow on my shoulders, I turned and trudged toward Chris and the boys. I climbed in the van and sat there as Chris started the ignition and slowly pulled away. I looked back to where I had stood minutes earlier, and I watched the very man who was going to bury my son come out from under a tree. He approached the opened ground with a shovel in his hand. I choked back a sob.

------------

The final gathering in honor of my son was scheduled for August 11, 2008. My family, along with many loving friends, poured into the chairs that were awaiting their arrival as a sweet woman from my church played her cello. When all were seated, we began the memorial with prayer.

I had no eulogy for Isaiah's memorial. What are you supposed to say about a life that was fifteen minutes short? Well, I'll tell you. After the 23rd Psalm was read, I got up in front of all of those people and wept. I spoke of those beautiful fifteen minutes of life. I told them how special and perfect Isaiah was. I read a poem that I had found on the Internet; it spoke volumes on a mother's love for a child who had passed from her arms and how special that little one was, though they weren't together on earth. Then

I went back to my seat. I felt like I had given every drop of love and motherhood that I could give.

Once again, the pastor gave a beautiful speech. The three songs—those I had picked out a few nights earlier as I sat rocking in my darkened living room—were played. They were songs of hope and the love of our Lord. It was absolutely beautiful. Extremely sad, but perfect.

Isaiah was honored and remembered.

# Chapter 12

When I arrived home, people surrounded me with love, phone calls, dinners, and the most beautiful sympathy cards. I knew they loved me and hurt for me, but they just didn't "get it" through no fault of their own. They slowly trickled back to their own lives, leaving me with many thoughts and aches to carry on my own. I felt abandoned, and I locked the door to my heart. My loved ones were to be excluded. I suppose it was my way to survive. I wanted to be alone.

Alone.

I made myself comfortable in that cold, dark hole of despair. I needed to dwell on my tragedy. I wanted to consume my loss by inhaling and exhaling the pain, touching the emptiness, and tasting the tears of despair. Why?

I. Did. Not. Want. To. Miss. One. Piece. Of. My. Loss.

I needed to experience every drop. I needed to allow God to carry me through . . . when I was ready.

I would mother Isaiah in secret. I had a feeling of shame as I thought on little things that I wanted to do for him. Just because he was absent from my physical life did not mean that my natural instinct as a mother—to show love to and for my child—was also absent. I carried him within my womb for nineteen weeks and three days. As each day passed, I grew more aware of his personality. I bonded with my son. I fell in love with the daydreams I had of holding him, loving him, bringing him home from the hospital, and raising him.

My entire being had been transformed into a new person. A new woman. A new mother. All that I looked upon was different. I noticed the way a raindrop rolled off a leaf . . . maybe because I had so many tears roll off my cheeks in much the same way. I noticed the way ants carried loads of dirt upon their shoulders, the same way I had begun carrying a weight upon mine, building the new foundations of my life.

I would never be the same, but I knew deep down that I wanted to be better. I wanted to be a better wife. Mother. Daughter. Granddaughter. Sister. Aunt. Friend. Neighbor. I wanted to reflect the beauty that I knew God had for me.

There was no right or wrong way to grieve, as long as I continued to walk on the path that was straight and narrow. I knew that if I stayed on that path rather than wandering away on my own path, God would always meet me right where I was. Sometimes, I would follow Him, having enough strength to continue. Other times, I had to pitch a tent and camp out right where I was. I didn't want to go any farther. I needed more time to feel, breathe, and cry as I explored my loss. Being the gentleman that God is, He carried me through the mud and muck. As He continued to pave the way, I followed. My attire might be covered in stains, torn with holes, and wrinkled with doubt, but my tears would cleanse the stains and straighten the wrinkles, and His hands would mend the holes.

Though I am a handful of years away from the beginning, I have not forgotten how I got this far. I need no reminders. I live surrounded by them every day. I see Isaiah's smile when I sit and laugh with my boys. I see him run as I watch my boys play gleefully with one another. I feel his love as my husband holds me. I see his eyes when I look into the mirror. Isaiah is all around me. He consumes my thoughts. My heart. My soul. He is, and will always be, my precious son. The little boy I continue to hike with for miles upon miles, through mud and muck, until that day we meet again.

When it comes to keeping the memory of my son alive, I become a fierce mother—just as I am to the four precious boys that I care for and give a tender motherly love to on a daily basis.

I was his mama.

I AM his mama.

A mother doesn't stop being a mother upon her child's death. I know death can be a scary word, especially when speaking of an innocent baby, but it happens. I believe this world needs more compassion for parents who want to memorialize the life of a deceased child. For me, the world kept spinning, unmindful of my shattered heart. Some women, including myself, frantically search for each shard so that we can piece our hearts back together. It may take months or years before we gather the many pieces scattered abroad. Our hearts have taken on a new shape, but that one very special piece cannot be found. Our child is gone but somehow still remains here with us. We medicate that empty hole in our hearts by doing unique things. Whether it be that empty spot at the table, in the car, under the Christmas tree, or on the blanket watching fireworks, we always notice. Our hearts are marinated in the love that we are able to give. To fill that empty spot.

If you know someone who has suffered the loss of a child, there are simple things that you can do that show you care. Just to speak that child's name aloud brings an unspeakable joy to a mother/

father's heart. It says, "I have not forgotten, and I will continue to remember your child."You can even send a card on a birthday, due date, holiday, or any given day of the year. It is freely giving love and support without going out on a limb or making yourself feel uncomfortable. Any little thing that you choose to do will mean a great deal to the parents. It's the time that you took in expressing yourself to the one you love that really counts.

Have you ever thought about what love really is or what is the best way to show love?

The Oxford Dictionary states that love is "an intense feeling of deep affection."

I agree with the above definition. I loved that little boy more than my fingers can type in an expression to describe.

God had to forsake Jesus at the cross. He never asked me to do the same to my son.

No more feeling shameful.

No more hiding.

No more whispering.

No more giving excuses.

He was my little boy.

He IS my little boy.

It may be that I honor his memory by placing a toy baby chick on his grave at Easter, a pumpkin in the fall, a wreath during the Christmas season. Maybe it's as simple as baking and decorating a birthday cake in honor of his life. Those are examples of how I honor Isaiah and mother him, in private ways.

In more public ways, I created a blog and wrote my first post on Wednesday, January 7, 2009. My blog allowed me to take my pain, turn it into words, and create a picture for others to see how I was really doing. I felt safe, hidden, and free. Mothers from all over the world reached out their hands and hearts in support, and I began to feel like I fit in this world again. I was transformed through my loss, and each post in my blog captured my pain and hope. My spiritual healing came from God, and my day-to-day living became awakened as I wrote posts describing where I was at in my journey.

As I searched old blog posts, I noticed that I was writing directly to Isaiah in the beginning, but as time went on, I began to write in a more matter-of-fact kind of tone, as in "This is how I'm feeling" and "This is what you can do to acknowledge the life of my son."

The following is a short letter that I wrote to Isaiah on Tuesday, January 13, 2009:

These Were My Dreams For You:

> I had so many dreams for you, Isaiah. I wanted to see you crawl and take your first step. Instead, I saw you take your first and last breath. I wanted to see your excitement as you had your birthday parties with your family and friends. Instead, your family and friends came to your burial and memorial. I wanted to see your eyes light up on Christmas morning. Instead, all that lit up was your Christmas ornament surrounded by the lights on the tree. I wanted to see you ride bikes with your brothers. Instead, I sit and watch your brothers playing outside together, and I picture you

running after them with a big grin on your face. You have been the greatest loss of my life. People will never realize the depth of my pain and sorrow. I have so much love for you, and you're not here for me to hold on to, rock to sleep, or tuck in at night. I have so much to give, but I can't give it to you because you are not here with us. I pray and ask God to tell you how much we love you and miss you. I really pray that you can feel my love. My love for you grows every single day, even though you aren't here. That is real love, a love that can grow and grow from our souls. I believe that God allows us to keep that love connection no matter how far apart we are. I love you, Isaiah, and I'm so thankful that God made you my son and me your mommy!

I concluded the above post with the following verse:

God blesses the people who patiently endure testing. Afterward they will receive the crown of life that God has promised to those who love Him (James 1:12).

I have written four blog posts for each birthday that has passed thus far. As you read each one, you will notice that each is different. I believe that love grows with time, as does the knowledge of all that was lost, when you lose your child. Not only did my love grow deeper, but so did the pain caused by my son's absence. The following are the birthday posts that I had written before the publication of this book:

First Birthday, August 3, 2009

I made a cake for you today. I know that you would have loved blowing out your very first candle and getting cake all over your sweet little face. I told your brothers that you are going to be having a huge birthday party in heaven with Jesus! They got so excited. I said that you are going to be watching us with a huge smile on your face as we sing "Happy Birthday to You."

I will never forget your precious face. Your perfect little round cheeks. Your button nose. Your tiny soft hands. My heart was so full of joy when you were placed in my arms. You were perfect. You are perfect. My sweet little Isaiah. I think about you every day. You are a part of me and always will be. I love you more than words can express."

Second Birthday, August 3, 2010

Two years ago, you blessed my life with yours. You were gently placed in my arms. I was amazed by the detail in which God had formed every little part of you. You were perfect. From your little eyes, soft ears, and button nose, down to your slender fingers, long legs, and ten little toes. All that I could speak to you were the words, "I love you, Isaiah Christopher." I needed to know that you were hearing my voice until you couldn't hold on any longer. You did so well. You were so brave. A mother couldn't be more proud of her son than I am of you. You have transformed my life so deeply. I learned lessons in life that one can't learn by picking up a book or attending years of college classes. I learned how to love more deeply. To be thankful for the simple things that this world offers. Life that only God can knit. Love that penetrates the depths of the soul. I will never take for granted the fifteen minutes that we were given. I will never stop sharing your life with others. I ache to hold you in my arms again. I love you beyond the moon and stars. You are greatly missed, Isaiah. Happy birthday, son.

Forever loved,
Mommy

Third Birthday, August 3, 2011

My dearest Isaiah,

Today is a day that has become one of the hardest for me to face. For the last three years, my soul has emotionally and physically ached over losing you. From the moment your heart stopped beating, I let a piece of mine journey into the heavens with you. I refused to let you be without your mommy.

I often get up at the crack of dawn, open my windows, and listen to the birds chirping their beautiful songs. I gaze over the dew-covered grass, and I begin thinking of you. Thoughts of heaven travel around in my head. I sit and ponder all the ways that you have been enjoying heaven these last three years. There must be so much beauty, peace, and love surrounding you. I can only imagine.

I pull your picture close so I can see every intricate detail that God had formed so perfectly, so beautifully. My hands long to gently rub the back of your little head, just as a mother does when she cradles her newborn against her breast.

I count each little finger on both tiny hands, and I picture you holding up three little fingers after I ask how old you are today. I can just hear the precious words, "I'm thwee, Mommy!" I know that I would ask you the same question over and over again because of how sweet you would have sounded. I'm quite sure that you would have gone running through our home, full of excitement, telling your brothers that it's your birthday! What a sight that WOULD have been.

I may not be singing "Happy Birthday to You" as you sit at the table with your cake in front of you, but I know that your great-grandmother Eleanore has already sung it to you. She was known for her beautiful voice, always making one feel like the most important person in the world. Give her a hug for me.

I love you, Isaiah. I cannot express enough how special you are to me. You are a part of our family, and I will never let you be forgotten. There has not been a day that has passed without you filling my thoughts. I will never be the same.

I'll love you always . . .

Fourth Birthday, August 3, 2012

Isaiah,

As I sit and write this letter at the beginning of a new day (12:30 am), I realize that these were some of the last precious hours I was blessed to carry you deep within my womb. If I had only known how it would end, I would have been on that hardwood floor in my hospital room, pleading to the Lord to spare your life . . . but the Lord always knows what He is doing. He knew that my strength would have dissipated during the night if I had known that you and I were traveling to the end of our road here on earth. I never would have believed that this is how your life was going to end. Even after four years, I can still see that hospital room as if it were yesterday. I can still smell the scents that August brings with it as your birthday approaches. For the last four years, the month of August has brought new meaning into my life. It is a time that my heart aches for days as I wish that you were here with us. A time when I sit and watch your brothers play, wondering what you would be doing with them. I feel so sad when I think of what you missed in life, but as of late, I have been trying to look at your loss differently. I'm trying to make my heart realize how happy and whole you are with the Lord. I make myself see you smiling and laughing with Jesus, enjoying every experience of heaven. Your death has not been the end of you, but the beginning of life for eternity. You get to experience perfect peace and joy that I cannot touch until I am with you in the presence of the Lord.

It has taken me almost thirty-one years to grasp the beauty that surrounds this world. True beauty. I looked out my window a couple of days ago and watched the rain fall from the clouds. I then looked at the bush that had been growing all summer right before my eyes. It captured every raindrop as they quickly rolled and dripped from leaf to leaf. It reminded me of how the Lord holds my every tear. Then, I watched the rain run down the window, just like the tear drops that run down my cheeks when I cry for you. It was a beautiful moment. The Lord showed, through nature, that He holds it all. My tears/laughter, joy/sadness, you/me. Through Him, we are still together.

You lived more than fifteen minutes within my arms; you lived nineteen weeks and three days within my womb. You have given me joy and love that will carry me throughout the years and into eternity.

I love you, Isaiah Christopher Ross. Happy birthday, son.

Love,

Mommy

Another public way of sharing the life of my son has been through one of our local newspapers. A gentleman from my church, who writes for this newspaper, asked me if I would be willing to write an article and answer the question, "What is pro-life to you?" When I was asked this question, my heart began to race as my eyes filled with tears for that little boy who filled my thoughts. Immediately, I agreed to write that article. I had two hours to put together something that would make the reader think.

My article ran for two weeks straight. I like to believe that it saved some precious lives. Why did I do this? I personally know what a *fetus* looks like. Can I ask why our society has given such a merciless name to the unborn? I held the tiny body of my nineteen week, three day old son as his lungs were depleted of oxygen and his heart slowed to the last beats to be heard . . . EVER . . . before he left my arms to be delivered into the arms of his Heavenly Father. He was anything but a faceless fetus. He was as human as they come. A precious boy, fully developed.

In certain areas of our own country, abortions are allowed at all stages of pregnancy. The "rules" of abortion state differently, but I personally know someone who knows otherwise. Abortion procedures are being conducted as you read this. Little lives are being taken because it has been allowed. I wonder how many women would choose life if they were allowed to participate in an abortion—if they viewed the horrific act of the murder of a child.

I did not have an abortion, but I had to go through an induced labor to save my life. My doctor did all she knew possible to save a life. Isn't that what we are supposed to do? It's my prayer that the loss of Isaiah's life will make a difference in lives across the world and even change the way a mother views her unborn child in an early stage of pregnancy. Every life that is taken—or shall I say murdered—loses out on a lifetime. A life that should only be taken by the God that knit the little one in the womb. I only wish that I had had the chance, the choice, to save the life of my son. The next time you are asked, "What is pro-life to you," what will your answer be?

To sum up all of the above, I would have to describe the periods of grief as being so intense at times that it's like watching vibrant fireworks explode in the darkened sky and feeling the bursts in your chest. As the thoughts come swimming in, you can literally feel the pain build within the walls of your chest. You don't just bury your child and move on. You bury your old life and make a new one, building memories of your child along the way, in any way you can think to do so. In the beginning, it can be brutal, and through enough passed time, you have built a new comfort zone to reside in. You are made new and will never be the same again. With a loss so great, how could you be? I will never be the same as I was before I endured the heartbreaking task of saying goodbye to my child. Through the loss of my son, I became a better person.

After blogging for four years and connecting with many women along the way, I connected deeply with Kelly Gerken, founder and president of Sufficient Grace Ministries. She was the second woman to reach out to me as I shared my heart online. She was there through every post, encouraging me every time I wrote. Our friendship grew as we both encouraged other women who were struggling with their own losses. In October 2012, I invited her and the vice president of Sufficient Grace Ministries to come to my hometown. The three of us put on a conference where women came and had fellowship together, remembering our children who had passed but speaking of the beautiful hope we have in the Lord, knowing that our precious children are safe and experiencing the greatest love ever known.

A few months after the conference, Kelly had asked me if I would consider being the Northern Michigan Regional Coordinator for Sufficient Grace Ministries! I replied with a humble "YES!" At the time of accepting, I was also offered the chance to study through an online website called Stillbirthday.com. After ten weeks and seventy hours of training, I was certified as an SBD doula. I am able to go alongside women who are going through a healthy pregnancy (live birth), and I can also support the mother who has learned that her child has passed, or will shortly after birth. For me, it's not only about supporting the mother but also knowing that I have traveled the journey that she is about to embark on and understand what she is going through. Had I not experienced the loss of a child, I would not have chosen this career/ministry path. The loss of my son has changed me, and in a way, my life has become his legacy.

God always uses our ashes to bring beauty. He will get the final word.

# CHAPTER 13

As I survived days, weeks, months, and years after the loss of my son, I suffered from a guilt that was extremely heavy at times. The first year was torturous in so many areas. I faced the firsts of all holidays, birthday, and other special events without him. On top of that, I tracked the time in which he would be doing all of his firsts. First tooth, smile, crawl, step, bite of big people food, etc. It had all been lost so that I could live. I was haunted, day in and day out, by how and why he died.

One Sunday morning, I was standing in the bathroom with my eight-year-old son, Parker, as I tidied his hair for church. As he stood and watched me in the mirror, he asked, "Mom, how did Isaiah die?" I kept combing his hair, and my heart began to race. Honestly, I was at a loss for words. How was I supposed to answer this question? A person may say, "Tell the truth." It's really not that easy. "Well, Parker, your brother's life was taken so that I could have a fighting chance at life. Yes, that's right, kind of like murder." Really?

I don't want to lie to my children. They need to know the truth but are far too young to completely understand the entire story. They know that I almost died, but I don't think their minds can imagine a little boy, their brother, lying in my arms, fighting for his life, heart slowly beating, oxygen depleting, death overtaking life . . . gone.

I think he saw the pain in my eyes and accepted my quick answer. "Parker, there are a lot of things about the loss of Isaiah that you can't understand right now at your age. When you get older, you'll be able to understand the story completely," I said as I continued combing over the same patch of hair a dozen times. He accepted my answer quickly and cheerfully and ran off to play with his brothers.

Sometimes I feel I have to conceal the way Isaiah died, as if I'm going to be judged on what a selfish, wretched mother I must have been to allow death to take my little boy. On rare occasions, my mother will have to comfort me, saying, "Jenny, you were going to die; the doctor did all she could to try and change your health, and there was no other option." With a crack in my voice, I conclude, "I know, I just wish . . ."

The summer of 2012, I went to the hospital to get copies of my medical records. Only a couple of people knew that I had requested the very papers that held my past. I ordered from the night of August 2, 2008 - August 5, 2008. The woman told me that I couldn't get them for a few days and that I could have them mailed or I could pick them up. "Pick up, please," I quickly stated. I opened the door, walked down the shadowed hallway, passed the cream-colored walls, and arrived at the elevator. My legs felt heavy, as did my heart. I pushed the button to the main floor, all the while focused on thoughts that consumed every inch of healing that had occurred over the last three and a half years. Had I just made a decision that I'm going to regret? Am I going to read the doctor's notes and find reason to believe that she was wrong in the decisions that were made regarding my health?

After three long days, I got a call from the woman in the medical records department. My papers were in an envelope and could be picked up at any time.

After retrieving the envelope, I sat in my car, still debating whether I should read my records or shred them. I started the ignition, laid the envelope on my lap, and slowly drove home, lost in my thoughts. If mistakes had been made, did I really want to know? Would the information in that envelope affect the healing I'd experienced up until then? However, my need to know was stronger than the desire to protect my heart. I had to read those records.

Back at home, I sat on the couch and carefully opened the seal of the envelope . . . the seal of "life." Slowly pulling out the packet of papers, I flipped through pages upon pages of blood transfusions. My past was alive again.

I continued searching and found what I was looking for—my doctor's medical notes. I read through them and found these poignant quotes:

> "The patient was adamant she wanted to try and save the pregnancy."
>
> "The decision in light of the chronic placenta abruption underlying an acute further abruption now leading toward DIC."
>
> "The decision was made to proceed with induction for life saving measuring."
>
> "The infant was then swaddled and wrapped in a warm blanket and placed on mother's abdomen . . ."
>
> I'm going to cut in here to say that Isaiah was delivered into the mighty hands of God at this point in the notes.

"Estimated blood loss during delivery is 525 mL."

I'm now in the OR.

"She was placed under anesthesia by Dr. O."

"Attempt at using the large curette to scrape free the tissue, but was very difficult."

"The placenta came out in multiple small fragments with pieces of membrane and small pieces of cord and very attached to the uterine wall."

"I had a very difficult time getting any kind of uterine wall texture."

"She was taken immediately to ICU."

"Estimated Blood Loss: 300-350 mL of active blood in the operating room."

"Fluid Replacement: 2300 mL in the operating room."

These were just little pieces of the 48 pages of copied notes from my medical records. I investigated every single letter and number in that booklet that held my life, my son's life. I had to see with my own two eyes, read each word . . . that there was no other option.

I placed that packet back into the white envelope and sat silently on my couch. Tears flooded my eyes as I whispered, "There was *no other option*."

I believe that, in that very moment, I was allowed a different kind of healing.

I had held myself captive in the first three years following Isaiah's death. I would emotionally and mentally keep my heart in the very place where his stopped. Swallowing the truth of his death was not an option for me. Until now.

No more.

No more imprisoning myself with unreasonable guilt. God's will is not for me to travel as if I were lost but to awake to a new day, finding the good, searching out love, and clinging to the hope that I have in Him.

I have concluded that there will be no forgiving myself. How do you forgive yourself when there was nothing you could do? It's neither possible nor necessary. I have come to accept that fact. Trust and faith in God will be the greatest ointments for my healing.

I made a decision to look at life deeper, for him . . . for me. I learned how to carry him in my heart instead of that blood-ridden bed, where the last of his heartbeats was heard.

I remember that in the first few months after his death, I would hide my smile from people other than my family. I thought if they witnessed a smile on my face, they would assume that I was "fixed." All better. *Now we can have her back . . . the way she used to be.* There was one problem with that. I would never be the same. And I didn't want anyone thinking otherwise.

To be honest, I don't think that I can go two hours without thinking about Isaiah. I carry him around in my heart, mind, and soul. He is a part of me. His little body was carved with special pieces of my husband and myself. The Lord knit him with the very best pieces of his daddy and me. I tell myself that is why he couldn't stay here on this earth. He was far too perfect.

# CHAPTER 14

Having had other children before Isaiah, the loss was even more apparent and deep for me. Every day, I watch my boys grow and develop their own unique personalities. I knew what a great loss Isaiah was . . . is. I lost a lifetime with him.

When I sit and contemplate the loss of my son, I can't help but wonder if this is the way that it was supposed to have been. I will never have the complete answer, but I know that I trust wholly in the Lord. Sometimes, I wonder about asking God for His will to be done. Will I trust Him fully, or will I only be willing to accept the circumstances that seem to get better with a quick fix? I feel that when bad things happen, we tend to pull away from God. In reality, it is the "bad" things, the hard trials, that bring us closer to Him. I don't want to walk away. I want to travel my journey following the footsteps that the Lord has already spoken into existence for my life. In a way, I am still very close to Isaiah, though he resides in heaven. We are both held in the arms of the Lord, just in two different lands. I await here in the earthly lands, and he dances around the Promised Land.

Isaiah never got to smile and laugh with us, but he also will never have to experience tears from sorrow and heartache. He never got to experience the warmth of the sun on his skin here on this earth, but he has endless rays of glory shining from the Son beaming upon him in heaven. He has been delivered from all harm and agony, brought into complete safety, love, and joy.

Isaiah wasn't a piece of property that I gave away. It's okay to say his name. To talk about him. It makes me happy. Yes, I may feel sad at times, but how could I ever be offended when you speak of one of my most precious jewels? If a diamond were crushed into many pieces, would it still appear beautiful? Of course it would. It's really all in how you look at it. You may not be able to wear that diamond on your finger, but you would find a different way to display the jewel—that being in many small ways. You couldn't put the pieces together, but you could accentuate each piece in different ways. That is how I mother my son. My life shattered into incalculable fragments at his death, but I still carry those fragments around with me every single day. I find ways to share his life with others. He mattered to me, and always will, until my dying day. His life accomplished more in fifteen short minutes than most people accomplish in a lifetime. Most people are concerned with only themselves, which ends up only changing personal areas that affect their very breath. Isaiah's very breath taken touched many lives and changed who I am as a whole. He wasn't just a baby; he was my son.

After having my dreams ripped from my heart . . . from my arms . . . I refused to believe that God would not bless us with another child. My husband and I consistently prayed for God to knit a precious child within my womb. I don't even think that I asked. I begged.

Why did I want to experience pregnancy so soon after burying my child? To be honest, the loss falls into a separate category than that of having your dreams of mothering a child in your arms, fresh from the surroundings of your womb.

When Isaiah died, my life shattered. I couldn't bring him back, no matter how many tears I continually cried or how much I pleaded with the Lord. He was gone.

I had been robbed of many joys. Rubbing my cheek along his soft delicate baby cheeks. Feeding and changing him every two hours for nights that would have seemed endless. Introducing my handsome bundle to my family and friends.

In a way, it was as if he never existed. I walked around with a swollen belly that appeared to be with child, though it was empty.

I knew that there was no guarantee that we would conceive another child, BUT . . . God blessed us yet again. I knew that having another child would not heal the pain of losing Isaiah, but it filled that spot in me that was silently screaming. Empty, but slowly being filled with hope.

Oh, how my heart leaped when my eyes witnessed that pastel pink line travel along the result window on the pregnancy test. I remember feeling like I was walking atop the clouds. I felt like I had redeemed my motherhood. I had been given this blessing six months after losing Isaiah.

I had an emotional roller coaster ride ahead of me. Many ups and downs, but God saw me through each one. During my fifth week, I began having pain in my abdominal area—the very same feeling that I had experienced when carrying Isaiah. I remember dropping my boys off at school before dialing my doctor's office as I sat in my vehicle. They made me an appointment to come in that same hour to perform an ultrasound. I started the ignition and began to drive carefully through a snowstorm. As I was driving, I began sobbing, begging God to spare this child's life. I made my request known unto God in the loudest form of speaking possible.

After arriving at the doctor's office, I was taken to a room where an ultrasound machine sat against a wall. It felt like I was reliving my loss all over again. The on-call doctor pulled the machine close and began the procedure. The exact same thing was happening in this pregnancy as I had experienced six months prior. There were blood clots forming around the amniotic sac that held my healthy, growing child. I was terrified! I not only wanted to escape another loss but to escape the same kind of loss—the kind where I fall deathly ill, an innocent child has to be born too early to survive, and I fight for my life. The appointment ended with little hope for a healthy baby. I made an appointment to see my doctor the following week.

The days slowly trickled by as I awaited my appointment. As the ultrasound was being conducted, silence filled the room. There was no heartbeat to be found. My heart sank. My soul was crushed. Why? My doctor told me how sorry she was to have to tell me this heartbreaking news, and she scheduled me for a D&C in one week. She mentioned that I might miscarry within that time. The next day, I began bleeding. I was bleeding heavily, so my husband took me to the ER. They told me that I was experiencing a miscarriage.

On the drive home, I could feel life inside of me. I could feel my child still hanging on. I refused to believe what my eyes had seen, what my ears heard. When I got home, I went into my bedroom, shut the door, and began praying. I prayed with power from the depths of my being, the prayer of a mother who simply can't bear to say goodbye to another child. I remembered the rainbows that appeared after Isaiah died. I believed that it was a promise that God made to me—to never allow the loss of another child in my life.

I made another appointment to be checked before my D&C was scheduled. I prayed with every ounce of my being. As the ultrasound brought up a picture of my child on that black and white screen, you could see a tiny heart fiercely beating.

God heard!

God answered!

There was still fresh blood forming into clots, but I chose to believe that God had given life. People around the world began to pray. On their knees. In the morning. Throughout the day. At bedtime. Spreading the word.

Our child began to grow, kick, and suck his thumb. The blood clots began to go away! We found out that we were having another little boy. How wonderful! Each week, I was blessed to watch my belly grow.

On the morning of October 16, 2009, we were preparing for his birth. I had this weight of fear on my shoulders. Fear of death. Is my child going to be born alive? Is my body going to be able to handle another birth? Another surgery? I prayed unceasingly.

At 9:21 a.m., my baby took his first breath of life as I exhaled the cloud of death that had consumed my thoughts and took my first breath of hope.

I felt like I had regained a piece that had been stolen from my body, my motherhood, and had another chance to fill my arms again. This was also a very emotional time for me, but I chose joy above all else. God had knit a child within me to bring not only a special healing but also trust that He holds the whole world. We named this little boy Ezekiel Isaiah Ross. Through Ezekiel's middle name, we were able to keep Isaiah's memory alive, honored, and spoken.

As I sit and ponder the purpose for each of my children who have blessed my life, I am filled with many warm thoughts. I would like to believe that each special son—Caleb, Devon, Parker, and Ezekiel—was placed in my life to bestow a purposeful motherhood upon me surrounded with endless hugs, kisses, and "I love you's." When I place Isaiah among the circle of sons, I meditate on the precious gift of his life. Maybe his life served to give me the gift of appreciation for life and God's beauty that surrounds us. I can choose to see the beauty.

We are not put on this earth for the pleasures of this world. After so many heartbreaks in my life, God has shown me a different way to look at life. To view His creation in a unique, intimate way. One way that really hit me during the beginning of my own loss was the very loss of His Son, Jesus. My son had his life taken to give me life. God's Son had his life taken to give us all life. My story cannot come close to the holy gift of our Lord, but the realization of how grand the gift of salvation is has made my thankfulness multiply dramatically.

I have chosen to live the life I have been given. You may ask, "Well, do you really have a choice?" The answer to that question is simple. About two years after losing Isaiah, I added a new element to my life. It's called living on purpose. I have to choose on purpose to smile. To laugh. To love. To live my life to the fullest. To not let the gift of my son be in vain. How would that be honoring to him?

When I gaze at a beautiful flower, I don't see only the colorful petals; I look into the very depths of where that flower first began. I see every detail etched into God's creation. I breathe the scent a little more deeply, not only for myself, but also for my son. When I view a sunset, the very masterpiece painted across God's magical canvas, I look a little more intently at every single detail, not only for myself, but also for my son.

I will never get over the loss of my son, but I will get through it. His life has not only affected my life in a powerful way, but it has imprinted an eternal love within every fiber of my being.

When I think back on that fun activity from first grade, I smile, knowing that the Lord fulfilled the dream that I had written out all of those years ago. *Mom* had been scribbled in crayon along that dotted paper. A mother. That was all I wanted in life, and that is what I am. A mother to five precious boys. I never dreamed that I would live through the loss of a son, but just as I had written my dreams of motherhood back in the first grade, the Lord was writing the story of my life. He is the author and finisher.

God of glory—have your glory.

Until we meet again, I will keep Isaiah's memory alive. I'm beyond thankful to be called his mother, and he, my son. I love you, Isaiah Christopher Ross.

> For whether we live, we live unto the Lord; and whether we die, we die unto the Lord: whether we live therefore, or die, we are the Lord's (Romans 14:8).

# Resources

Sufficient Grace Ministries at
*http://sufficientgraceministries.org*

Website created by Sherokee Ilse at
*http://www.babiesremembered.org*

Website created for all types of loss at
*http://www.stillbirthday.com*

Still Standing Magazine at
*http://stillstandingmag.com*

Compassionate Friends at
*http://www.compassionatefriends.org/home.aspx*

# NOTES

1. Chapter 2: "Be fruitful, and multiply" (Genesis 1:28).

2. Chapter 3: March of Dimes: *http://www.marchofdimes.com*

3. Chapter 3: "Now faith is the substance of things hoped for, the evidence of things not seen" (Hebrews 11:1).

4. Chapter 3: "What time I am afraid, I will trust in thee" (Psalm 56:3).

5. Chapter 4: Definition for disseminated intravascular coagulation (DIC): *http://tinyurl.com/prpqa5e*

6. Chapter 4: Definition for placenta accreta: *http://www.mayoclinic.com/health/placenta-accreta/DS01203*

7. Chapter 4: "In my distress I called upon the Lord, and cried to my God: and he did hear my voice out of his temple, and my cry did enter into his ears" (2 Samuel 22:7).

8. Chapter 11: "The Lord is good, a strong hold in the day of trouble; and he knoweth them that trust in him" (Nahum 1:7).

9. Chapter 12: The Oxford Dictionary, definition of love.

10. Chapter 12: "God blesses the people who patiently endure testing. Afterward they will receive the crown of life that God has promised to those who love him" (James 1:12, NLT).

11. Chapter 14: "For whether we live, we live unto the Lord; and whether we die, we die unto the Lord: whether we live therefore, or die, we are the Lord's" (Romans 14:8).

For more information about

**Jennifer Ross**

*&*

***Isaiah's Story***

please visit:

*http://jenniferross777.wordpress.com/*

*sgmjenniferross@gmail.com*

*@JenniferRoss777*

*https://www.facebook.com/AuthorJenniferRoss*